NAKED PUTS

POWER STRATEGIES FOR CONSISTENT PROFITS

ERNIE ZERENNER & MICHAEL CHUPKA

Marketplace Books
Columbia, Maryland

This book, along with other books, is available at discounts that make it realistic to provide them as gifts to your customers, clients, and staff. For more information on these long lasting, cost effective premiums, please call us at 800-272-2855 or e-mail us at sales@traderslibrary.com.

ISBN: 1-59280-330-X

ISBN 13: 978-1-59280-330-9

Printed in the United States of America.

TABLE OF CONTENTS

FOREWORD

WHY YOU HAVE TO READ THIS BOOK!

This is your complete A-Z guide to naked puts, an income-generating stock options investment strategy. Selling naked puts is a conservative income-generating strategy that allows investors to earn premium on bullish and neutral stocks and is the best strategy to acquire stock at a discount. This is not a book for those who are interested in trading options as a speculative investment vehicle.

Both authors have had the benefit of talking to thousands of options investors over the last 10 years. This work includes the ideas, concepts, fortunes and misfortunes of investors' experiences trading the naked put strategy. Its purpose is to help you succeed in the use of the naked put options strategy. It is a practical guidebook that is rich with illustrations, theoretical and real life examples.

Many books on options explain the techniques of this strategy, but then do not help in the management of the position once it is established. We have tried to go further and help you understand how to manage the position no matter what direction the stock might turn. It is very important to have a plan and know how to execute it, especially if the position goes against you. Sometimes your trades will not follow the path you hoped; therefore, you need an approach to address any eventuality. We have given you a complete approach to manage your positions as each expiration approaches.

As a result of reading this book you should expect to:

- Gain enhanced concepts of options.

- Learn general and specific rules for researching naked put trades.

- Determine which stocks are most suitable for the strategy.

- Learn techniques for analyzing and comparing potential trades.

- Learn focused criteria to help select the best trade for your goals.

- Discover steps on how to place the trade and common mistakes to avoid.

- Gain management techniques and exit strategies for any situation.

For illustrative purposes, graphics from the PowerOptions web site (www.poweropt.com/npb/) are used throughout the text. When you have completed your reading, you will not be restricted to using the web site to make trades, although it is a powerful and useful tool to consider. It serves here as a means to help analyze and compare options data and demonstrate management techniques. This web site continues to be an invaluable tool for us in our own investing.

The only magic formula for options, or any other kind of trading and investing, is knowledge. You need a clear-cut understanding of your strategy: how to apply it, how to manage it, and how to discipline yourself so you use it—every day.

NAKED PUTS

POWER STRATEGIES FOR CONSISTENT PROFITS

Chapter 1

AN INTRODUCTION TO OPTIONS AND THE NAKED PUT STRATEGY

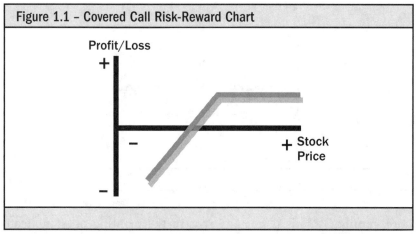

Figure 1.1 – Covered Call Risk-Reward Chart

Profit/Loss

Stock Price

Source: PowerOptions (www.poweropt.com)

DOES THIS IMAGE LOOK FAMILIAR? If you have ever researched or traded options, you are probably familiar with the *covered call* strategy and the *risk-reward* chart. An investor who applies to trade options through a brokerage firm is allowed to trade covered calls as a Level I investor. This is because covered call investing is arguably the most conservative options strategy an investor can use in a portfolio to increase returns, add protection, and generate income.

If you have researched the various options strategies, you might also be familiar with the broker's common warnings on trading *naked puts*: "Well, that is about the riskiest thing you can do, trading naked puts." In order to trade naked puts, your brokerage house may require you to apply for a higher level of options investing. This reserved and outdated concept is somewhat troubling to intermediate and advanced options investors. Why? Well, let's take a look at the risk-reward chart for a naked put trade:

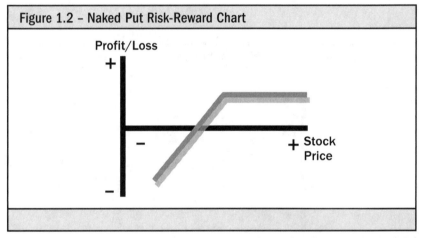

Figure 1.2 – Naked Put Risk-Reward Chart

Source: PowerOptions (www.poweropt.com)

Look familiar? This is not an error in the printing or a duplicate image. Naked puts, the strategy that you have probably been warned away from researching, have the same risk-reward tolerance as covered calls. As you can see by the charts, the maximum risk in trading the naked put or the covered call strategy is if the stock drops to a value of $0.00. This, of course, is the same risk an investor has when buying shares of stock. However, when investors trade the naked put strategy, they will collect a premium up front to hedge the position.

Even if the shares drop to a value of $0.00, the naked put investor would have fared better on the trade over the investor who simply bought shares of the same stock.

So, why might your broker tell you that naked puts are one of the riskiest things you could trade? One answer may be lack of knowledge. Your broker may know that a form of investing called *options* exists, though he or she may have never traded them. It is possible that your broker does not know the specifics of the various options strategies that can be used to help protect and build your portfolio value.

Another answer might simply be knowledge: The knowledge your broker might not want you to have because your broker knows if you are a more informed and educated investor, you will not need his or her services. It is widely held that, on average, investors who are educated in options-trading strategies are more adept at researching stocks and analyzing the market.

Kopin Tan, a respected columnist who writes for *Barron's* financial newspaper once wrote: "…options investors who trade options tend to be more independent, risk-tolerant, richer, and better educated than those who don't." This statement was based on a study performed by Harris Interactive as commissioned by the Options Industry Council. The article, titled "A Special Breed, Typical Option User: Richer, Smarter, Independent," states that those options investors surveyed "are more likely to personally research investments; are less reliant on stock and mutual funds; and are keener to learn about new ideas and vehicles."[1]

Tan continues on to say that 71 percent of those surveyed who do not trade options say they do not understand options, despite the

---

1. Reprinted with permission of Dow Jones and Company, Inc, Licence number 1863850064458

increase in educational tools and information that has become available during the last several years. Of those surveyed who do not trade options, 30 percent say they feel options are "too risky" and would not consider venturing into that investing arena.

There are risks in trading options, just as there are risks in trading stocks or mutual funds. These risks can easily be managed once the investor has the proper knowledge regarding the investment vehicles. Options can be used by speculators to increase leverage and gamble on higher-risk, potentially higher-return strategies. However, investors can also use options in a very conservative way to generate income and protect against market declines. The naked put strategy is in the more conservative camp of options investing strategies.

This book is designed to help you obtain that knowledge so you can become a more educated options investor, specifically regarding the naked put strategy. This text will also showcase one of the premier internet tools available to help you find, compare, and analyze these investments: PowerOptions.

Before we get into the specifics of the naked put strategy, we should first define the different types of options and the rights, obligations, and requirements of these very powerful trading vehicles.

OPTIONS DEFINED

Options are contracts that give investors the right, but not the obligation, to buy or sell shares of stock. Investors can trade these contracts just as they can buy or sell (short) shares of stock. Each option contract typically represents 100 shares of the underlying security, therefore, if an investor purchases one option contract, the investor is purchasing the right to buy or sell 100 shares of the underlying security; five option contracts would represent 500 shares.

There are two types of options used by investors: *calls* and *puts*. Buying a call option gives the owner of the contract the right, but not the obligation, to buy shares of stock at a set price (called the *strike price*) at any time before the option expires (called the *expiration date*). Buying a put option gives the owner of the contract the right, but not the obligation, to sell (force someone to buy) shares of stock at a set strike price prior to the expiration date. These definitions apply to investors who purchase options speculating that the stock will rise or fall to make a profit. On the other side of these transactions are *options sellers*. Selling a call obligates the investor to deliver shares of stock at the strike price to the option buyer. Selling a *put* obligates the investor to buy shares of stock at the strike price.

Table 1.1 – Option Rights/Obligation Chart

	Buyer	Seller
Call	Owns the right to buy shares of stock from the call seller.	Obligated to deliver shares of stock to the call buyer.
Put	Owns the right to sell shares of stock to the put seller.	Obligated to buy shares of stock from the put buyer.

Strike Price

Each optionable stock will have several strike prices the investor can choose from to buy or sell for both calls and puts. In the case of a call buyer, the strike price represents the price of the stock that the call buyer has the right to purchase shares of stock from the call seller. If the stock price is trading above the strike price of the call, the option is in-the-money (ITM). The call buyer can *exercise* the call contract, buy shares of stock at the strike price, and then sell the shares at market for the higher value. The call seller would have to deliver shares of stock at the value of the strike price, to fulfill the obligation, even though the market is offering a higher price. If the

Figure 1.3 – Option Chain - Stock XYZ trading at $51.00

Strike	Call Sym			Put Sym	
Officemax Inc. (OMX) $ 52.05		MAY Expiring 5/19/2007 25 days left			
40.00	OMXEH			OMXQH	
42.50	OMXEV			OMXQV	Out of the Money Puts:
Option Strike Prices: 45.00	OMXEI			OMXQI	(Strikes Below Stock Price)
47.50	OMXEW	In the Money Calls:		OMXQW	
50.00	OMXEJ	(Strikes Below Stock Price)		OMXQJ	
52.50	OMXEA			OMXQA	
55.00	OMXEK	Out of the Money Calls:		OMXQK	In the Money Puts:
60.00	OMXEL	(Strikes Above Stock Price)		OMXQL	(Strikes Above Stock Price)

Source: PowerOptions (www.poweropt.com)

stock price is trading below the strike price of the call, the option is out-of-the-money (OTM). If the call option is OTM at expiration, the call would expire worthless. The call buyer would not exercise the right to buy shares of stock at the strike price when the stock could be purchased at a lower value.

Put options have the opposite requirements of call options. Please see Figure 1.3 for a visual example. A call buyer owns the right to purchase shares of stock, whereas a put buyer owns the right to sell shares of stock. A put buyer is a bearish investor, as the put will gain in value as the underlying security falls in price. For a put buyer, the strike price represents the value that the investor can force the put seller to buy shares of stock. If the stock is trading below the put strike price, the put is ITM, the opposite from the call scenario. If the stock is trading below the put strike price, the put buyer can force the put seller to buy shares of stock at a higher value than the current market price. If the stock is trading above the strike price, the put option is OTM and will expire worthless. The put buyer would not exercise the right to sell shares of stock at the strike price if the shares could be sold at the market for a higher value. Table 1.2 is a quick summary of these terms.

Table 1.2 – ITM/OTM Quick Chart

	In-the-Money	Out-of-the-Money
Call	Stock price above the strike price.	Stock price below the strike price.
Put	Stock price below the strike price.	Stock price above the strike price.

Expiration Date

The owner of the contract, whether it is a call or a put, has a set time frame to exercise this right before the option expires. This is known as the expiration date. Standard stock equity options expire on the third Friday of the specific expiration month. Technically, options expire on the third Saturday of the specific expiration month, but the last day that investors can actively trade, close, exercise, or assign their options is the third Friday. Some index options may expire on the morning of the third Friday or the third Thursday afternoon. Recently, some indexes have released weekly options and some Exchange Traded Funds (ETF's) have released quarterly expiration options. This text focuses on the standard expiration, those options that expire on the third Friday of every month.

Each optionable stock will have various expiration months the investor can choose to buy or sell. These different months are referred to as the *option series* for that stock. There are three possible expiration series for an optionable stock:

> **JAJO** - January, April, July, October
> **MJSD** - March, June, September, December
> **FMAN** - February, May, August, November

Regardless of the expiration series, every optionable stock will have the near month and the next month available. The example in Figure

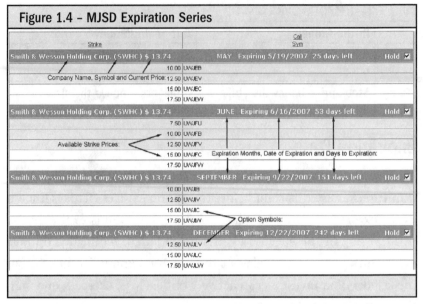

Figure 1.4 – MJSD Expiration Series

Strike		Call Sym
Smith & Wesson Holding Corp. (SWHC) $ 13.74	MAY Expiring 5/19/2007 25 days left	Hold ☑
10.00	UWJEB	
Company Name, Symbol and Current Price: 12.50	UWJEV	
15.00	UWJEC	
17.50	UWJEW	
Smith & Wesson Holding Corp. (SWHC) $ 13.74	JUNE Expiring 6/16/2007 53 days left	Hold ☑
7.50	UWJFU	
10.00	UWJFB	
Available Strike Prices: 12.50	UWJFV	
15.00	UWJFC	Expiration Months, Date of Expiration and Days to Expiration:
17.50	UWJFW	
Smith & Wesson Holding Corp. (SWHC) $ 13.74	SEPTEMBER Expiring 9/22/2007 151 days left	Hold ☑
10.00	UWJIB	
12.50	UWJIV	
15.00	UWJIC	
17.50	UWJIW	Option Symbols:
Smith & Wesson Holding Corp. (SWHC) $ 13.74	DECEMBER Expiring 12/22/2007 242 days left	Hold ☑
12.50	UWJLV	
15.00	UWJLC	
17.50	UWJLW	

Source: PowerOptions (www.poweropt.com)

1.4 shows the MJSD series; but, since the March and April expiration dates have already passed, May is listed as the near option. In figure 1.4, you can see that the July and August options are not yet available, but the options with those expiration dates will be released once the next expiration date passes.

At the time of this publication, 40 percent of the more than 3,000 optionable stocks, indexes, and ETF's also have LEAPS™ options available. LEAPS are *long term equity positions* and have a January expiration date one or two years out in time. During the months of May through July, the near term January LEAPS shift to regular contracts and a new series of LEAPS one year more out in time are released.

TRADING OPTIONS

Like shares of stock, option contracts are listed on the exchanges with a *bid* price and an *ask* price. An option buyer will pay the value of the listed ask price. An option seller will collect a premium at the bid price. The market maker for the underlying security determines the bid and ask prices for each option. The difference between the bid price and the ask price is referred to as the *bid-ask spread*. The market maker can manipulate the market by setting the bid-ask spread wider apart. The market maker earns money by purchasing contracts at the bid price and then selling them to the public at the ask price.

The bid-ask spread also prevents investors from buying large amounts of contracts and selling them quickly, as this would cause an immediate loss on the position. Without the spread in place, it is possible that investors could manipulate volume by buying large amounts of contracts, then selling them right away without penalty.

Figure 1.5 shows the bid-ask spread for calls and puts on a given stock. For the 50 strike call, the bid price is $1.15 and the ask price is

Strike	Call Sym	Opt Bid	Opt Ask		Put Sym	Opt Bid	Opt Ask
Officemax Inc. (OMX) $ 49.22		MAY Expiring 5/19/2007 19 days left					Hold ■
37.50	OMXEU	11.60	11.90		OMXQU	0.00	0.05
40.00	OMXEH	9.10	9.40		OMXQH	0.00	0.10
42.50	OMXEV	6.70	7.00		OMXQV	0.00	Put Bid - 0.10
45.00	OMXEI	4.40	4.70		OMXQI	0.20	Ask Spread 0.30
47.50	OMXEW	2.50	2.65		OMXQW	0.75	0.90
50.00	OMXEJ	1.15	1.30		OMXQJ	1.85	2.00
52.50	OMXEA	0.40	0.50		OMXQA	3.60	3.80
55.00	OMXEK	0.10	0.15		OMXQK	5.80	6.00
60.00	OMXEL	0.00	0.10		OMXQL	10.70	11.00

Figure 1.5 – Stock XYZ Trading at $49.50, 19 Days to Expiration

(Call Bid - 4.70, Ask Spread .2.65, Ask Spread 1.30 annotations shown in figure)

Source: PowerOptions (www.poweropt.com)

$1.30. This spread makes it impractical for any investor or group of investors to buy a large number of contracts at the ask price and then sell them immediately, as they would incur a $0.15 loss. The bid-ask spreads for the 50 strike put and the 47.5 strike put are also $0.15.

Since each contract represents 100 shares of the underlying security, the total cost to buy an option would be:

[Option Ask Price * Number of Contracts * 100]

In the above example, the ask price for the 50 strike call is $1.30. One contract would cost the option buyer $130 (plus commissions):

[Option Ask Price * Number of Contracts * 100]
$1.30 * 1 * 100 = $130 (plus commissions)

The investor pays $1.30 for each share that is represented by the contract. If an investor purchased 5 contracts, it would cost $650; 10 contracts would cost $1,300.

For the 50 strike put, the ask price is $0.90. An investor buying one contract would pay $90 (plus commissions), 5 contracts would cost $450 and 10 contracts would cost $900 (plus commissions).

Option Pricing Components

The option premium has two components, *intrinsic value* and *time value*.

Intrinsic value refers to the amount of monetary value the strike price of the option is ITM. As noted earlier, a call option is ITM if the stock price is trading above the strike price. For an ITM call, the intrinsic value equals the current stock price minus the strike price (if the stock price is greater than the call strike price).

The put option is ITM if the stock price is below the strike price of the option. For an ITM put, the intrinsic value equals the strike price minus the stock price (if the stock price is less than the put strike price).

Figure 1.5 shows that the 47.5 call has an ask price of $2.65. If XYZ is trading at $49.50, the 47.5 strike option is two points ITM, or has $2.00 of intrinsic value. Remember, a call buyer is purchasing a contract with the right to buy shares of stock at the value of the strike price. Since the 47.5 strike call is below the current stock price, the option seller must collect at least the intrinsic value of the option in order for the trade to be fair.

Why would the option seller agree to give up shares of stock for less than the current market value? If option sellers could only receive $1.00 to give other investors the right to buy their shares of stock for $2.00 less then the market price, no one would trade options. This is why the option premium must at least equal the intrinsic value of the option strike price.

The same philosophies apply to the put option. In Figure 1.5, the 52.5 strike put has an ask price of $3.80. Since XYZ is trading at $49.50, the 52.5 strike put is three points ITM, or has $3.00 of intrinsic value. A put buyer is purchasing the right to sell shares of stock at the value of the strike price. The put seller, who is obligated to buy the shares of stock, must collect at least the intrinsic value for the trade to be fair.

Why would put sellers agree to buy shares of stock for a higher price than the current market value if they did not receive adequate compensation?

OTM options do not have intrinsic value. The premium for OTM options is comprised completely of *time value*.

Time Value refers to the dollar amount the option buyer is paying for the time to expiration and the dollar amount the option seller is collecting for the time to expiration.

In the above example:

Stock XYZ is trading at $49.50.
The 47.5 call has an ask price of $2.65.
The 47.5 call is two points ITM ($49.50 – $47.50).
The remaining $0.65 is the *time value* for that option.

The $0.65 represents the premium the call buyer pays for the right to buy shares of stock anytime during the next 19 days. This means that the call buyer is paying slightly more than $0.03 per day for the right to buy the shares of XYZ at $47.50 per share ($0.65 time value / 19 days remaining to expiration = $0.0342 per day).

For the 52.5 strike put:

Stock XYZ trading at $49.50.
The 52.5 put has an ask price of $3.80.
The 52.5 put is three points ITM ($52.50 – $49.50).
The remaining $0.80 is the *time value* for that option.

The $0.80 represents the premium the put buyer will pay for the right to sell shares of stock during the next 19 days. Here we see the put buyer is paying slightly more than $0.04 per day for this right ($0.80 time value / 19 days remaining to expiration = $0.0421 per day).

For OTM options, the listed price is the time value for that option. In Figure 1.5, the ask price for the 52.5 strike call is $0.50. Remember, the 52.5 call is OTM because the stock is trading below the strike price. The 52.5 call has no intrinsic value. An investor who purchases the 52.5 call is speculating on a sudden rise in the stock to make a profit. If XYZ were still trading at $49.50 at expiration, the 52.5 call option would expire worthless. The call buyer would not exercise the right to purchase shares of stock at $52.50 when shares could be purchased directly on the market for less. If the call option expires worthless, the long call speculator would lose the full amount of the call purchase price.

In Figure 1.5, the ask price for the OTM 47.5 Put is $0.90. The put is OTM because the stock price is trading above the put strike price. An investor who purchased the 47.5 put is speculating that the stock will drop in price. If XYZ falls below $47.50, the put buyer can force the put seller to buy shares of stock for a higher value than the market price. If XYZ remains at $49.50 or rises, the 47.5 put will expire worthless. The put buyer would not exercise the right to sell shares of stock at 47.5 when the shares could be sold at the market price for a higher value.

As expiration day approaches, the time value on all options will decay. At expiration, any ITM options, whether they are calls or puts, will only retain their intrinsic value, and all OTM options will expire worthless as they no longer have any inherent value.

> **Trading Tip:** A common question for traders is: If investors buy or sell an option with a further-out expiration date, do they pay or receive more for that option? The answer is that options that are bought or sold further out in time will have a higher time value for the same strike price.

Figure 1.6 shows the XYZ chain again, this time with the *time value* and *percent time value* (the time value amount represented as a percentage of the underlying stock price) amounts shown for different expiration months. This figure shows that the time value for the May

| Figure 1.6 – Option Chain – Stock XYZ Trading at $49.50 |

Strike	Call Sym	Opt Bid	Opt Ask	Time Value	% Time Value	Put Sym	Opt Bid	Opt Ask	Time Value	% Time Value
Officemax Inc. (OMX)					MAY Expiring 5/19/2007 19 days left					Hold ■
37.50	OMXEU	11.80	11.90	-0.12	-0.2%	OMXQU	0.00	0.05	-	-
40.00	OMXEH	9.10	9.40	-0.12	-0.2%	OMXQH	0.00	0.10	-	-
42.50	OMXEV	6.70	7.00	-0.02	-0.0%	OMXQV	0.00	0.10	-	-
45.00	OMXEI	4.40	4.70	0.18	0.4%	OMXQI	0.20	0.30	0.20	0.4%
47.50	OMXEW	2.50	2.65	0.78	1.6%	OMXQW	0.75	0.90	0.75	1.5%
50.00	OMXEJ	1.15	1.30	1.15	2.3%	OMXQJ	1.85	2.00	1.07	2.2%
52.50	OMXEA	0.40	0.50	0.40	0.8%	OMXQA	3.60	3.80	0.32	0.7%
55.00	OMXEK	0.10	0.15	0.10	0.2%	OMXQK	5.80	6.00	0.02	0.0%
60.00	OMXEL	0.00	0.10	-	-	OMXQL	10.70	11.00	-0.08	-0.2%
Officemax Inc. (OMX)					JUNE Expiring 6/16/2007 47 days left					Hold ■
40.00	OMXFH	9.40	9.70	0.18	0.4%	OMXRH	0.05	0.15	0.05	0.1%
42.50	OMXFV	7.10	7.30	0.38	0.8%	OMXRV	0.20	0.30	0.20	0.4%
45.00	OMXFI	5.00	5.20	0.78	1.6%	OMXRI	0.55	0.65	0.55	1.1%
47.50	OMXFW	3.10	3.40	1.38	2.8%	OMXRW	1.25	1.35	1.25	2.5%
50.00	OMXFJ	1.80	1.95	1.80	3.7%	OMXRJ	2.35	2.50	1.57	3.2%
52.50	OMXFA	0.90	1.05	0.90	1.8%	OMXRA	3.90	4.20	0.62	1.3%
55.00	OMXFK	0.40	0.55	0.40	0.8%	OMXRK	5.90	6.10	0.12	0.2%
57.50	OMXFY	0.15	0.25	0.15	0.3%	OMXRY	8.30	8.50	0.02	0.0%
60.00	OMXFL	0.05	0.15	0.05	0.1%	OMXRL	10.70	11.00	-0.08	-0.2%

Source: PowerOptions (www.poweropt.com)

50 call (19 days left to expiration) is $1.15. The corresponding June 50 call (47 days left to expiration) has a time value of $1.80.

A call seller would collect an additional $0.65 of time value for 28 more days until the option reached expiration. Time value works for the option seller as the premium decays over time, meaning that time value works against an option buyer. Time value is the fee collected by the writer and the added cost that is paid by the option buyer.

Trading Tip: Notice in Figure 1.6 that the at-the-money (ATM) options, those closest to the stock price, have the highest time value of all potential strikes in a given month. The ATM strike will always have the highest time value in an options series.

REAL WORLD ANALOGIES

Let's look at a real world analogy to help define options. If you have read any articles or texts defining options before, this analogy may be familiar.

CALL OPTIONS

Your neighbor has decided to sell his house. He informs you that he is going to put his house on the market for $250,000. You have some money set aside and you feel you could buy your neighbor's house, make some improvements, and sell it for a profit or rent it out. But, you are not 100 percent ready to commit to this real estate purchase. So, you approach your neighbor.

"Hey Tom," you greet him one fine spring day while you are both mowing your respective lawns. "I am interested in purchasing your house. However, I am not sure if I have all my ducks in a row right now. I tell you what; I'll pay you $5,000 today if you agree not to sell your house to anyone else for the next 30 days. Between now and then, I will let you know if I can buy your house for the asking price of $250,000."

Your neighbor contemplates your offer. Under this agreement, he cannot sell his house for the next 30 days, but you have agreed to purchase his property at his asking price. If you decide not to purchase his property within those 30 days, he keeps the initial $5,000 (2 percent of his asking price). If you do purchase his property, he still keeps the $5,000 and collects the $250,000 asking price. Your neighbor agrees to your offer, you two draw up a contract, and you pay him the $5,000.

This is exactly how a call contract works. In this analogy, you are the call buyer. You have paid $5,000 (the option ask price) to obtain the right to buy your neighbor's house (the underlying stock) at a set price of $250,000 (the strike price) anytime within the next 30 days (the expiration date).

Call Buyer: The call buyer owns the right to buy shares of stock at the strike price at any time prior to the options expiration date. The call buyer will pay a premium for this right. A call buyer is a bullish investor, as the call option will appreciate in value as the stock rises. If the stock has moved in the desired direction, the call buyer can *exercise* his right and buy shares of stock at the strike price, *or* the call buyer can simply *sell to close* the contract and profit from the increase in value.

EXAMPLE TRADE – LONG CALL

You have been tracking stock XYZ that is currently trading at $50.00 per share, and you feel it may appreciate a few points within the next 30 days. You could simply purchase 100 shares of XYZ for a total cost of $5,000 plus commissions. Your potential profit is unlimited and your maximum risk is the amount of money you paid to enter the position. Or, you could purchase a call giving you the right to buy 100 shares of XYZ at $50.00 within the next 30 days for a fraction of the cost of stock ownership. The call option trade, called a *long call*, would look like Figure 1.7.

Breakdown:

- You have purchased the right to buy shares of XYZ at $50 (the strike price) anytime within the next 30 days.

- Your maximum profit is unlimited, as the stock could rise infinitely. As the stock rises, the intrinsic value of the option will increase as well.

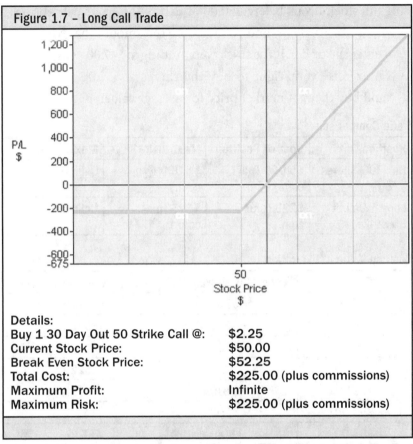

Figure 1.7 – Long Call Trade

PP/L
$

50
Stock Price
$

Details:
Buy 1 30 Day Out 50 Strike Call @: $2.25
Current Stock Price: $50.00
Break Even Stock Price: $52.25
Total Cost: $225.00 (plus commissions)
Maximum Profit: Infinite
Maximum Risk: $225.00 (plus commissions)

Source: PowerOptions (www.poweropt.com)

- Your *break even* is equal to the **Strike Price + Total Cost.** If the stock is trading at $52.25 at expiration, you could *exercise* your right to buy shares of stock at $50.00 and then sell the shares at market price, or you could *sell to close* your contract for its intrinsic value of $2.25.

- Your maximum risk is equal to the price you paid to enter the position (*option ask price* plus commissions).

If the stock drops below $50.00 at expiration, your call option will *expire worthless*, and you will lose the amount that you paid to enter the trade. If the stock were trading at $47.00, why would you exercise your right to buy the shares at $50.00 when you could buy them at market price for a lesser value?

Trade Comparison

Position	Cost of Position	Max. Risk	Max. Profit
Buy 100 Shares XYZ	$5,000 (plus com.)	$5,000 (plus com.)	Unlimited
Long 1 Call at 50 Strike	$225 (plus com.)	$225 (plus com.)	Unlimited

Position Value at Expiration

Stock Price at exp.	Long 100 Shares XYZ	Long 1 Call at 50 Strike
$47.00	−$300	−$225
$48.00	−$200	−$225
$49.00	−$100	−$225
$50.00	$0	−$225
$51.00	+$100	−$125
$52.00	+$200	−$25
$53.00	+300	+$75

Although the absolute profit value of the long call position is lower compared to owning the shares of stock, the percentage return of the initial investment is much higher.

If the stock were trading at $53.00, the return on stock ownership would equal:

Total Profit/Total Cost = $300/$5,000 = 6%

The return on the long call trade would equal:

Total Profit / Total Cost = $75 / $225 = 33%

Since the long call position had a much lower initial investment, the position is leveraged, thus you are able to achieve a higher percentage return in comparison to owning the shares of stock. This is the primary reason speculators use options to increase their rate of return.

How does this relate to the contract you have purchased from your neighbor Tom? Let's say that during the 30-day holding period, you hire a professional to survey Tom's land. During that survey, the professional discovers a small gold deposit in the back of Tom's yard. The estimated value of the lot is now more than $1,000,000!

Tom is ecstatic when you tell him the news. He can now sell his property for four times his initial asking price.

"But," you remind him, "I have a contract with you giving me the right to purchase your house for $250,000 within the next 15 days. I think I will exercise that right and buy your house for the contracted amount."

Tom is now less ecstatic. He is going to receive his asking price of $250,000 and he will keep the $5,000 you paid him for the contract, but he is going to miss out on the extra appreciation of his property due to the recent discovery.

In this real estate analogy, your neighbor Tom is the call seller.

Call Seller: The call seller is obligated to deliver shares of stock to the option buyer at the strike price anytime prior to the options expiration date. The call seller will collect a premium for this obligation. A call seller is a bearish investor if the underlying stock is not owned (called *naked call* trade). If the underlying stock is owned, the call seller is neutral to bullish (called *covered call* trade). If the stock rises, the call seller must deliver shares of stock at the strike price, or the call seller can avoid *assignment* by buying to close the obligation.

EXAMPLE TRADE – NAKED OR SHORT CALL

You have been tracking stock XYZ that is currently trading at $50.00 per share, and you feel it may depreciate a few points within the next 30 days. You could short (sell) 100 shares of XYZ and collect $5,000 minus the cost of commissions. Your potential profit is limited to the amount of money you collect for shorting the stock. You will only retain the full amount if the stock is trading at $0.00, but you could achieve a profit if the stock is trading at any price below $50.00. Your maximum risk in this trade is unlimited as the stock could theoretically continue to rise.

Instead of shorting the stock, you could sell a call contract obligating you to deliver shares of XYZ at a price of $50.00 within the next 30 days. This call trade is called a *naked call* or *short call* trade (Figure 1.8).

Breakdown:
- You have sold an obligation to deliver shares of stock you do not own at $50 (the strike price) within the next 30 days. Your maximum profit is limited to the initial premium you collected. You will keep the entire profit if the stock is trading below $50 at expiration.

- Your break even is equal to the **Strike Price + Premium Received**. If the stock were trading at $52.10 at expiration, you would be forced to deliver shares of stock at $50.00. Since you do not own the shares, you would have to purchase the shares at $52.10 then sell them for $50.00. This

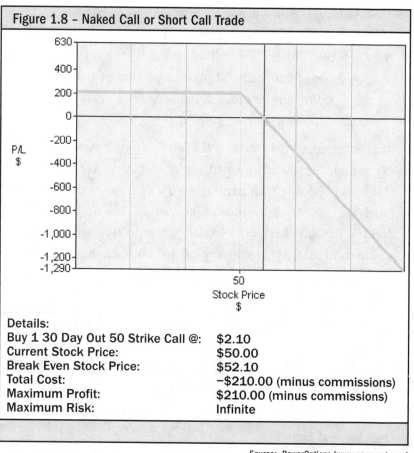

Figure 1.8 – Naked Call or Short Call Trade

P/L
$

Stock Price
$

Details:
Buy 1 30 Day Out 50 Strike Call @: $2.10
Current Stock Price: $50.00
Break Even Stock Price: $52.10
Total Cost: −$210.00 (minus commissions)
Maximum Profit: $210.00 (minus commissions)
Maximum Risk: Infinite

Source: PowerOptions (www.poweropt.com)

would give you a loss of $2.10, but you would still keep the initial premium you collected.

- Your maximum risk is infinite as the stock can rise to any value. If the stock is trading at $100 at expiration, you will have to purchase the shares at market price and deliver them at $50.00, fulfilling your obligation. In this scenario, your loss would be: $100 (cost) − $50.00 (obligation) − $2.10 (premium) = loss of $47.90 per share.

- Although you did not have to purchase shares of stock, your broker would require you to have available in your account either the full obligation amount ($50.00 * number of contracts * 100) or a portion of that amount, depending on the broker's requirements. This amount is called the *margin* requirement.

Just as the long call trade, if the stock drops below $50.00 at expiration, the naked call will expire worthless as well. Since this is the opposite transaction and the call was sold instead of purchased, the trade would be successful. The option expires and the investor keeps the initial premium received. No one would want to buy shares of stock at $50.00 when they could buy them at the market price for a lesser value.

Trade Comparison

Position	Cost of Position	Max. Risk	Max. Profit
Short 100 Shares XYZ	−$5,000 (plus com.)	Unlimited	$5,000 (minus com.)
Short 1 Call at 50 Strike	−$210 (plus com.)	Unlimited	$210 (minus com.)

Position Value at Expiration

Stock Price at exp.	Short 100 Shares XYZ	Short 1 Call at 50 Strike
$47.00	+$300	+$210
$48.00	+$200	+$210
$49.00	+$100	+$210
$50.00	$0	+210
$51.00	−$100	+$110
$52.00	−$200	+$10
$53.00	−$300	−$90

When investors short shares of stock, they are looking for a drop in the stock value. Shorting shares of stock means investors are agreeing to deliver shares of stock they do not own, essentially borrowing shares of stock from their broker. If the stock falls, the investor can buy the shares of stock at the lower price to cover the obligation of the short trade. In the above example, if an investor shorted 100 shares of XYZ at $50.00 and the stock fell to $47.00, the shares could be purchased on the market at the lower price, and the short obligation would be covered. The investor would profit $3.00 per share on the trade. If the stock goes up in price, the investor would have to buy shares of stock at the higher price to cover the short position. The risk on this position is infinite as the stock could continue to rise.

Selling a call without owning the underlying shares is a similar trade. Investors sell the right to deliver shares of stock they do not own. If the stock falls, the call will expire worthless and the call seller will keep the initial premium. If the stock rises call sellers will have to deliver shares of stock they do not own to fulfill the obligation.

Put Options

Put options have the opposite rights and obligations of call options. However, that definition is a little vague and does not paint a clear image of the contract. The best way to understand put options is to think of them as insurance for shares of stock.

In this analogy, let's say that several things went exactly as you had planned this year—with a few extra bonuses thrown in. You saved enough to go comfortably forward with your financial goal from the last three years: the two-seat convertible sports car with all the special features, custom interior, and heated seats (for when you must have the top down on cooler days). You place the order with the dealership and pick up your new beauty a couple weeks later.

Now you have to consider your insurance policy. For the past several years you had been paying a low premium for liability only and a low deductible. That will not cut it anymore. Your new car needs full coverage for any possible scenario, including getting caught in an alien tractor beam, if your insurance company offers that kind of coverage. As you are driving through town, top down of course, you see a bright neon sign on top of one of the buildings: "BBBB Auto Insurance—You have the need to drive, we have the drive to fit your needs."

Since you have the need, you pull into the parking lot and walk into the small office with the brown shag carpeting.

"Big Bob will be with you in one minute," the secretary informs you.

"Big Bob?"

"Yes, of Big Bob's Blatantly Basic Auto Insurance."

You take a seat on a plastic blue chair, which seems a bit sticky. Just as you begin to second-guess your impulsive curiosity, Big Bob appears from the back office, starts to shake your hand vigorously and before you know it, you are now seated in his office across from his desk.

"What can Big Bob do for you today?"

You reluctantly explain your situation. After listening to your needs, Big Bob outlines a few policies.

Policy I – Big Bob's Big Special: Full and unconditional coverage for the complete value of your new car, *plus* 20 percent of that value for any damages caused by all natural or unnatural events, including any mechanical damages caused by EGGF—External Galactic Gravitational Force (tractor beams). Cost per month: Astronomical, 20 percent of your car's value.

Policy II – Big Bob's Basic: Full coverage for the complete value of your new car with some standard clauses stating that if the value of your car ever went up in price, you would still only be covered for damages equaling the value of your car at the time the insurance policy was signed. Cost per month: 5 percent of the total value of the new car.

Policy III – Big Bob's Bargain: Coverage for 20 percent of the value of your new car if any damage occurs from natural or unnatural causes. Cost per month: 0.8 percent of the total value of your new car.

Big Bob smiles wide as he starts to pitch Policy I again. You stop him before he can continue on and silently review Bob's offers.

Policy I has all of the protection you need, but at 20 percent of your car's value per month! After five months, you would have paid Big Bob the total value of your new car and you still would have about 60 months of payments left! Even though it offers Bob's EGGF coverage, Policy I is not for you.

Policy II gives you full coverage for the value of your car, but after 20 months you would have paid Bob the full value of your car and you would still need to cover the car for another 40 months. Policy II does not fit your budget either.

Policy III has a more reasonable premium, but it only covers your car for 20 percent of the total value.

At this point you might decide to leave the offices of Big Bob and research other companies' policies for coverage.

Regardless of which policy seems the most appealing to you, this is exactly how put options work for stock investors and speculators. Investors that own shares of stock can purchase a put to protect their shares of stock from a decline in value just like car owners use insurance to cover their vehicles.

Think of the car in the above analogy as 100 shares of a $50.00 stock that you have purchased. To protect those shares against a large decline, you could purchase a put option, giving you the right to sell your shares at a set price. This strategy is referred to as a *protective put*.

If you wished to cover the entire purchase amount of your stock plus 20 percent of that value, you could purchase an ITM 60 strike put. This would give you the right to sell, or force someone to buy your shares of stock at $60.00 any time between now and the expiration date. In order to reserve that right, you would have to pay at least the intrinsic value—in this example $10.00—plus the time value. No one would sell you the right to sell your shares of stock for a higher value than its current price without adequate compensation. This ITM protective put strategy is just like Big Bob's Big Special Policy I.

If you simply wished to cover the total cost of your stock, you would purchase the ATM 50 strike put. There is no intrinsic cost for this protection. However, the put might still cost $2.00 or $3.00 per contract. If the stock dropped below $50.00 per share, you could force someone to buy your shares for your initial purchase price. In order to have this protection, you might have to pay $2.00 or $3.00 per month, or 5 percent of the underlying price of the stock. This ATM protective put strategy is just like Big Bob's Basic Policy II.

If you expected the stock to hold most of its value but wanted some protection if the stock dropped for some unforeseen reason, you would purchase the OTM 40 strike put. If the stock suddenly tanked below $40.00, you could force someone to buy your stock at $40.00 per share, minimizing your losses. This might cost you $0.80 to $1.00 per contract, depending on the stock, and only covers your shares for a significant drop in price. This OTM protective put strategy is just like Big Bob's Bargain Policy III.

As detailed previously in this chapter, the put option increases in value when the stock price falls. A put buyer could also be speculating on a drop in the price of the stock, but does not wish to short the stock. The investor is bearish on the underlying security so would not purchase shares, either. The investor simply wishes to profit from a down-trending stock. The put contract gives the investor a leveraged trading vehicle to profit on a bearish stock.

Put Buyer: The put buyer has purchased the right to sell, or *put* (force the put seller to buy) shares of stock at the strike price anytime prior to the option's expiration date. Just like the call buyer, the put buyer will pay a premium for this right. The put buyer is a bearish investor, as the put option will appreciate in value as the stock declines. If the stock has moved in the desired direction, the put buyer can *exercise* his right and force someone to buy the shares of stock at the strike price, *or* the put buyer can simply *sell to close* the contract and profit from the increase in value.

EXAMPLE TRADE – LONG PUT

You have been tracking stock XYZ that is currently trading at $50.00 per share and you feel it may depreciate in value within the next 30 days. Since you are bearish on XYZ, you could short

100 shares of XYZ or you could sell a 50 strike call as outlined above. If you are very bearish on the stock and are expecting a large decline in price, you can purchase a put option that will yield a higher potential profit if the stock does fall. Figure 1.9 is an example of the long put trade.

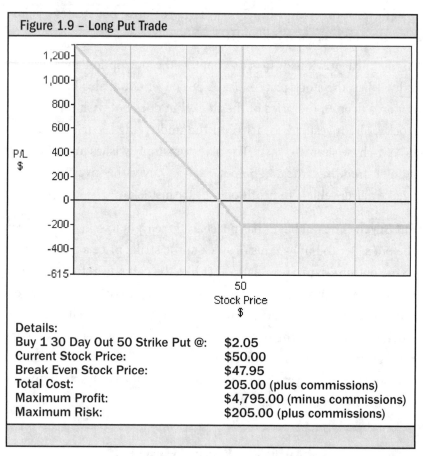

Figure 1.9 – Long Put Trade

Details:
Buy 1 30 Day Out 50 Strike Put @:	$2.05
Current Stock Price:	$50.00
Break Even Stock Price:	$47.95
Total Cost:	205.00 (plus commissions)
Maximum Profit:	$4,795.00 (minus commissions)
Maximum Risk:	$205.00 (plus commissions)

Source: PowerOptions (www.poweropt.com)

Breakdown:

- You have purchased the right to force someone to buy shares of stock at $50.00 (the strike price) within the next 30 days.

- Your maximum profit is the strike price minus the premium paid (ask price). Since the stock cannot drop below $0.00, the potential returns are not unlimited as they theoretically are with the long call purchase.

- Your break even price is equal to the **Strike Price – Total Cost**. If the stock is trading at $47.95 at expiration, you could *exercise* your right to force the option seller to buy shares of stock at $50.00, or you could sell to close your contract for $2.05.

- Your maximum risk is equal to the price you paid to enter the position.

If the stock rises above $50.00 at expiration, your put option will *expire worthless,* and you will lose the amount that you paid to enter the trade. If the stock were trading at $53.00, why would you exercise your right to force someone to buy your shares of stock at $50.00 when you could sell them at market price for a higher value?

Trade Comparison

Position	Cost of Position	Max. Risk	Max. Profit
Short 100 Shares XYZ	−$5,000 (plus com.)	Unlimited	$5,000 (minus com.)
Long 1 Put – 50 Strike	$205 (plus com.)	$205 (plus com.)	$4,795 (minus com.)

Position Value at Expiration

Stock Price at exp.	Short 100 Shares XYZ	Long 1 Put - 50 Strike
$47.00	+$300	+$95
$48.00	+$200	-$5
$49.00	+$100	-$105
$50.00	$0	-$205
$51.00	-$100	-$205
$52.00	-$200	-$205
$53.00	-$300	-$205

Again, although the profit value of the long put seems lower in comparison to shorting the shares of XYZ, the percentage return is much higher.

If the stock were trading at $47.00, your return on the short stock position would equal:

Total Profit/Total Cost = $300/$5,000 = 6%

Your return on the long put would equal:

Total Profit/Total Cost = $95/$205 = 46%

Since the long put position had a much lower initial investment requirement, the position is leveraged, thus you are able to achieve a higher percentage return in comparison to shorting the shares of stock.

If the stock had risen during the 30-day expiration period, the put option would expire worthless. In the above example, if the stock had risen to $53.00, the put buyer would not exercise the option. As mentioned earlier, why would the put buyer force someone to buy shares of stock at $50 when the put buyer could sell the shares at market price for the higher value? If the put option expires worthless, the put buyer has only lost the premium initially paid to enter the position.

Using long puts as a protective strategy against shares of stock that you own is just like using a *stop loss*. You do have to pay for the protection the put contract offers, but the put offers a better protection for your stock. Stop losses do not protect your shares from gap downs in after-hours or pre-market trading. The fall in the stock will break right through your stop loss without any effect. With a protective put in place, you would still be able to force someone to buy your shares anytime prior to the expiration date.

Put Seller: On the other side of the transaction is the put seller. Think of the put seller as Big Bob from the real world analogy. The put seller is offering "peace of mind" to the investor who wants to protect shares of stock or is attempting to profit from a recent decline.

The put seller is obligated to buy shares of stock at the strike price anytime prior to the options' expiration date. The put seller will collect a premium for this obligation. A put seller is a bullish investor who wants the stock to rise in value. If the stock is trading above the sold put strike price, the option will expire worthless and the investor will keep the premium. If the stock falls below the strike price, the investor will be forced to purchase shares of stock at the strike price fulfilling the obligation of the put contract. The put seller can avoid *assignment* by *buying to close* the obligation.

EXAMPLE TRADE – NAKED PUT

Back to XYZ again, and this time you feel the stock will rise above $50.00 within the next 30 days. Since you are bullish on

XYZ, you could buy 100 shares of XYZ or you could buy a 50 strike call as outlined in the first example. Investors could also sell a put contract on XYZ obligating them to buy shares of stock if the stock is trading below the strike price at expiration. If the stock remains above the $50.00 strike price, the put contract will expire worthless and the investor will keep the premium. Figure 1.10 is the *naked put* trade.

Breakdown:

- You have sold an obligation to buy shares of stock at the strike price of $50.00 if the stock is trading below that price at expiration.

- Your maximum profit is equal to the initial premium received at the time of sale.

- The break even price is equal to the **Strike Price – Premium Received.** If the stock were trading at $48.10 at expiration, the investor would be forced (assigned) to buy shares of XYZ at $50.00. The investor could then sell the shares at market price for a loss of $1.90. The investor still keeps the initial premium of $1.90, so the trade is a wash.

- Your maximum risk is equal to the break even price. Since the stock cannot drop below $0.00 in value, the naked put trade does not have an infinite risk like the naked call position.

If the stock stays at $50.00 or above, the put option will expire worthless. The put buyer would not force the put seller to buy shares of stock when they could be sold on the market for a higher value. The risk in this strategy is if the stock drops significantly or if the company declares bankruptcy. If the stock dropped

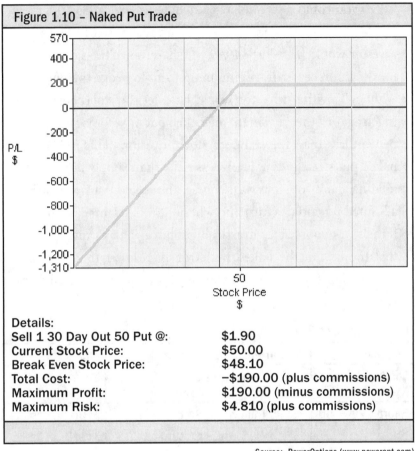

Figure 1.10 – Naked Put Trade

Details:

Sell 1 30 Day Out 50 Put @:	$1.90
Current Stock Price:	$50.00
Break Even Stock Price:	$48.10
Total Cost:	−$190.00 (plus commissions)
Maximum Profit:	$190.00 (minus commissions)
Maximum Risk:	$4.810 (plus commissions)

Source: PowerOptions (www.poweropt.com)

to $0.01, the naked put investor would be forced to buy shares of stock at $50.00 to fulfill the obligation. The investor would incur a loss of $49.99, *however*, the investor would still keep the initial premium for selling the put. In this example, if the stock fell to $0.01, the investor would have lost $48.09 per share. This is a significant loss. But consider in comparison the loss of an investor who simply bought shares of XYZ at the same time.

The stock investor would have purchased shares at $50.00, then would have seen those shares drop to a value of $0.01. The stock investor would have lost $49.99 per share, since the stock investor did not receive any premium up front to hedge the position. Although neither investor would have let the stock decline so much against their position, the naked put investor is risking 2.2 percent less than the standard stock investor. This is why the naked put strategy is actually less risky than simply buying and holding shares of stock. Of course, the naked put investor has a limited potential return and will not take advantage of profits if the stock appreciates drastically in price. This example shows that the risk in the naked put strategy is lower than outright stock ownership, despite the warnings you may have heard from various brokers.

Trade Comparison

Position	Cost of Position	Max. Risk	Max. Profit
Long 100 Shares XYZ	$5,000 (plus com.)	$5,000 (plus com.)	Unlimited
Short 1 Put – 50 Strike	–$190 (minus com.)	$4,810 (plus com.)	$190 (minus com.)

Position Value at Expiration

Stock Price at exp.	Long 100 Shares XYZ	Short 1 Put – 50 Strike
$47.00	–$300	–$110
$48.00	–$200	–$10
$49.00	–$100	+$90
$50.00	$0	+$190
$51.00	+$100	+$190
$52.00	+$200	+$190
$53.00	+$300	+$190

The naked put position allows an investor to take advantage of a neutral to bullish market sentiment without buying shares of stock. The table shows that if the stock moves up significantly in price, the naked put investor will only make the initial premium that was received. If the stock falls in price, the naked put investor will lose less monetarily compared to a long stock investor due to the premium received that hedges the position.

As stated before, your broker will not allow you to simply sell the put option without having some capital available to cover the obligation of the short put position. If the investor wished to be totally cash-secured to cover the obligation, the investor would have to have funds available equal to the maximum obligation. In this example, that obligation would equal $50.00 * number of contracts * 100. If one contract was sold, the obligation would be:

Strike Price * number of contracts * 100 =
$50.00 * 1 * 100 = $5,000

Although the investor has not purchased shares of stock, the *margin requirement* must be available through the expiration time frame of the sold put. Although some brokerage firms may require only a percentage of the total requirement to be available, it is more conservative to be totally cash-secured when trading naked puts (more on this in Chapter 2.)

The naked put strategy allows the investor to collect a premium and profit on a neutral or bullish stock without owning the underlying shares. The investor is obligated to purchase shares of stock but *only* if the stock drops below the sold put strike price at or before the expiration date. Many investors use this strategy to generate income in their portfolios and to potentially buy shares of stock at a discounted price.

In the next chapter, we will discuss the different types of investors and methods they use when trading naked puts, the specifics behind the naked put strategy, as well as several aspects of the naked put trade that investors should embrace and potentially avoid.

Chapter 2

THEORY BEHIND THE NAKED PUT TRADE

AS MENTIONED IN THE PREVIOUS CHAPTER, the naked put strategy is a neutral to bullish investment. The strategy is profitable when the stock stays at the same price at the time of the trade or moves up in value before the option's expiration date. Unlike a stock investor or a long call investor, the naked put investor will not profit if the stock moves up significantly. The profits in this strategy are limited to the initial premium the naked put seller receives.

But before we move on, let's recap some specifics of put options from the previous chapter

- Put options can be bought or sold just like shares of stock.

- Just like shares of stock, put options fluctuate in price.

- A put contract typically represents 100 shares of an underlying security.

- A put seller is obligated to buy shares of stock; A put buyer has purchased the right to sell shares of stock.

- Investors who sell (write) put options have various strike prices to choose from. The strike price represents the price the investor is obligated to buy shares of the underlying stock.

- Put options have a set time frame when the put buyer can exercise the right to force the put seller to buy shares of stock, called the expiration date. Equity options typically expire on the third Friday of each month. Each optionable stock will have several expiration months that the investor can choose to buy or sell put options.

- A put seller (writer) will collect a premium for selling the contract, called the bid price.

Now that we know the basics of put options, let's review our specific naked put strategy.

Action: Sell to open (write) puts against a researched security.

Purpose: To earn income on a bullish stock without purchasing shares outright.

Reward: The premium received for selling the contract.

Reward Achieved: When the stock stays above the strike price of the sold put at expiration.

Obligation: To buy shares if the stock drops below the strike price.

Risk: Stock drops to $0.00 or a significant amount below the strike price.

WHO TRADES NAKED PUTS?

Well, any investor who has the knowledge of the specifics of the trade and who also know the benefits, advantages, and risks of the naked put strategy: Ernie Zerenner and Michael Chupka, the authors of this text, as well as other members of the PowerOptions staff; clients of the PowerOptionsApplied Stratium TradeFolio; and hundreds of thousands of investors all around the world.

Investors who implement the naked put strategy in a portfolio can be broken down into two categories: First, those investors who use naked puts to buy shares of stock at a discount (referred to as Group 1 investors throughout the remaining text) and second, investors looking to earn a profit on a bullish or neutral stock without buying the underlying shares (referred to as Group 2 investors).

The first group of naked put investors is considered more conservative. These investors have thoroughly researched the underlying security and have a bullish sentiment on the security for the next 3, 6, or 12 months. At the current time, the stock might be slightly higher than their target price. Instead of buying the shares at the higher price, these investors will sell OTM puts over the expiration period hoping that the puts will expire worthless and that they will keep the premium. These investors can continue selling put contracts month by month, each time collecting a premium and lowering the overall cost basis. If the stock eventually falls below the strike price, the investor will buy shares of stock at a personal target price, though the overall cost basis of stock ownership will be lower due to the premiums received.

The second group is the more aggressive type of naked put investor. Investors in this group will find puts with a higher premium in order to get a higher return. The risk in this type of naked put investing is that stocks with higher option premiums tend to fluctuate in price more often (more on this later in this chapter). This means that the underlying security has a higher probability of dropping below the put strike price, causing potential losses for the investor.

WHY TRADE NAKED PUTS?

One of the advantages of this strategy is the premium the naked put seller receives hedges the position and lowers the potential risk. The premium gives the investor some protection if the stock were to fall below the put strike price prior to the expiration date. Take a moment and reflect back to the example in Chapter 1. If a stock investor purchased shares of XYZ at $50.00 and the stock dropped to $0.01, the stock investor realized a loss of $49.99. Meanwhile, the option investor who sold the $50.00 strike put for $1.90 would only have lost $48.09 on the trade. Because the naked put seller received cash up front, the total potential loss is less than owning the stock.

In some option strategies, this hedge is called *downside protection.* In a covered call trade, an investor will buy shares of stock and then sell a call against those shares. In the example from Chapter 1, if the investor had purchased 100 shares of XYZ at $50.00 and sold the 50 strike call for $2.10, the downside protection would have been 4.2 percent. The stock price could drop 4.2 percent, or $2.10 to $47.90 before the covered call investor would realize a loss on the trade. The downside protection is defined as how far the stock can drop before the investor is losing money on the position. In a covered call trade, this value is calculated as Option Premium Collected/Stock Price.

The naked put trade is an *uncovered position*, meaning the investor does not own shares of the underlying stock. The investor's obligation is the strike price of the put option, not the price of the underlying security at the time the trade was placed.

HOW DOES THE NAKED PUT MEASURE UP?

Investor A buys 100 shares of ABC at $24.00. Investor A's total cost, or risk, is $2,400 ($24.00 per share * 100 shares). Investor A has no downside protection, as he or she simply purchased shares of stock.

Investor B buys 100 shares of ABC and sells a 22.50 strike call and collects $1.85. Investor B's total cost, or risk, is $2,215 ([$24.00 per share * 100 shares] − [$1.85 premium * 1 contract * 100 shares per contract]). In this covered call trade, investor B has a downside protection of 7.7 percent ($1.85 premium / $24.00 cost per share). Investor B will not start to lose money on the position unless ABC falls below $22.15.

Investor C sells a 22.50 strike put against ABC and collects a premium of $1.00. Investor C's total risk is $2,150 ([$22.50 obligation price * 100 share obligation] − [$1.00 premium * 1 contract * 100 shares per contract]). The sold put obligates investor C to purchase shares of stock at $22.50, and the position is uncovered. Investor C's obligation and risk are based on the strike price of the sold put, not the cost of the underlying stock at the time of the trade.

Does this mean that Investor C only has 4.2 percent downside protection, since downside protection is calculated as Option Premium Collected/Stock Price ($1.00/$24.00)? Semantically, the answer is yes. However, this is not how the protection is calculated for the naked put position. Investor C does not have to purchase shares of ABC unless the stock drops below $22.50

per share. Investor C keeps the initial $1.00 premium regardless if the put option expires worthless or if the put is assigned, and Investor C is forced to buy shares of ABC at $22.50. Investor C's break even price on the naked put trade is $21.50 (Strike Price obligation minus Premium Received). Investor C will not start losing money on the position unless shares of ABC fall below the break even price. Since ABC is trading at $24.00, Investor C's protection is equal to:

Stock Price – Break Even / Stock Price =
(Where Break Even = Put Strike Price – Option Premium) =
$24.00 – $21.50 / $24.00 = $2.50 / $24.00 = 10.4%

For this naked put trade, shares of ABC can fall $2.50, or 10.4 percent of the current stock price before Investor C realizes a loss on the trade.

For the naked put strategy, the protection is called *percent to break even*. This is still defined as the percentage value the stock can drop before the naked put investor is losing value on the trade, or more simply, the percentage the stock can drop before it hits the break even point at expiration.

In the example from Chapter, 1 the investor had sold a 50 strike put on XYZ and collected a premium of $1.90. The sale of the put obligates the investor to buy shares of stock (have the shares of stock *put* to them) if the stock was trading below $50.00 per share at expiration. The put seller keeps the premium regardless if the option expires or if the put buyer exercises the option forcing the put seller to buy shares of XYZ. The percent to break even in the example from Chapter 1 is:

Stock Price − Break Even/Stock Price
(Where Break Even = Strike Price − Option Premium)
$50.00 − ($50.00 − $1.90) / $50.00
$50.00 − $48.10 / $50.00
$1.90 / $50.00 = 3.8%

The underlying security can drop as much as 3.8 percent before the investor is losing money on the position at expiration. This means that XYZ would be trading at the break even price at expiration, which in the example was $48.10.

If the stock was trading at $48.10 at expiration, the put would be assigned, meaning the option seller would be forced to buy shares of stock at $50.00. The investor could then sell the shares of stock at market price for a loss of $1.90 ($50.00 purchase price minus $48.10 current value per share). The investor still keeps the $1.90 for selling the put contract, thus the trade is a wash (not including commissions).

The example in Chapter 1 is an *At-the-Money* naked put trade because the put that was sold had a strike price equal to the stock price. If XYZ were trading at $51.00 per share and the $50 strike put was sold, the percent to break even would be:

Stock Price − Break Even / Stock Price =
(Where the Break Even = Strike Price − Option Premium)
$51.00 − ($50.00 − $1.90) / $51.00 =
$51.00 − $48.90 / $51.00 =
$2.90 / $51.00 = 5.7%

In this adjusted example, the break even price is still $48.10, but the stock price at the time of the trade was $51.00. This means XYZ can drop an additional $1.00 before it is trading at the break even price, an extra 1.9 percent protection over the original example in Chapter 1.

Trading Tip: In the original example from Chapter 1, the strike price of the sold put equaled the stock price thus the option was ATM. In the adjusted example above, the strike price of the sold put is below the stock price, and the option is OTM. Since there is a lower risk in selling the OTM put, it is unlikely that the investor would be able to collect $1.90 in premium for the $50 strike put if the stock was trading at $51.00. The listed bid price for the OTM option would be slightly lower.

Looking at an option chain, we can see that deeper OTM options offer greater protection, but the naked put seller would receive a much lower net premium.

Even though the OTM 40 strike put offers a 20.1 percent to break even, the bid price for the put option is only $0.05 (Figure 2.1). If the investor was selling only one or two contracts, the total amount received for selling the contracts would be $5.00 to $10.00. Depending on commission costs and brokerage fees, this small net premium might not be worth the effort to trade despite the high level of protection. In contrast, the ATM 50 strike put has a $1.40 premium, but only a 2.9 percent to break even.

Figure 2.1 – Option Chain showing Put Bid Price and Percent to Break Even

Strike	Put Sym	Opt Bid	% Break Even	
Alexion Pharma. Inc. (ALXN) $ 50.00	JUNE Expiring 6/16/2007 11 days left			Hold ☐
35.00	XQNRG	0.00	OTM Put Bid Price vs. % To Break Even:	-
40.00	XQNRH	0.05		20.1%
45.00	XQNRI	0.15		10.3%
50.00	XQNRJ	1.40	◄————————►	2.9%
55.00	XQNRK	5.10	ITM Put Bid vs, % to BE:	0.2%

Source: PowerOptions (www.poweropt.com)

Another advantage of the naked put strategy is that it is an uncovered position, as mentioned before, meaning that shares of the underlying stock are not actually owned. This is why it is referred to as a *naked put*. When an investor sells, or writes, a naked put he or she is entering into a contract to buy shares of stock at a set price. Investors would not usually purchase shares of stock and then sell a contract obligating them to buy more shares of stock at a lower price unless they were planning on accumulating a large amount of shares.

Although naked put sellers do not own shares of the underlying security, they will still be required to have funds in reserve to place the trade. A brokerage firm will not permit investors to enter into the put contract obligating them to buy shares of stock without having at least a portion of the total monetary requirement available. Most brokerage firms will require an investor to have 25 percent of the total contract obligation available in the account in case the stock is *put* to them, but each broker is different and your margin requirements may be slightly higher.

The Cash-Secured Naked Put

Because this is an income-generating strategy, many investors trade naked puts in tax-sheltered accounts, such as IRAs. In an IRA account, it is required that 100 percent of the total obligation be available in the account. This is called a *cash-secured* naked put.

Let's look at an example trade. In this example, we are going to sell to open 10 contracts of the 50 strike put of underlying stock XYZ.

Total Obligation: $50 (price you are obligated to buy shares of stock) * 10 (number of contracts) * 100 (shares represented by each contract) = $50,000, the same amount an investor would pay if purchasing 1,000 shares of XYZ. If the investor left $50,000 in reserve until the expiration date, the investor would be totally *cash-secured* on the position.

If the investor sold the naked put on margin, he or she would only need to have $12,500 (1/4 of the total obligation) on hold in the account to cover the obligation for selling the naked put.

Margin: In options trading terminology, *margin* refers to the amount of money an options seller will have to have on hold to cover the fulfillment requirements of the call or put. The term *margin* is also used to define the amount of money an options *credit spread* investor will have to have in an account to cover the position. Call or put buyers and options *debit spread* traders do not have margin requirements, as the risk on those positions is equal to the premium paid for the option or the *net debit* of the spread.

If investors sell a naked put on margin, they will potentially increase the overall return on the position compared to the naked put investors who are totally cash-secured. Let's look back to the example trade in Chapter 1 and compare the position if the put was sold on margin or sold cash-secured:

Table 2.1 – Cash-Secured Naked Put vs. Using Margin

	Premium Received	# of Sold Contracts	Total $ Received	Obligation	Funds on Hold	% Return
Cash Secured	$1.90	10	$1,900	$50.00	$50,000	3.8%
On Margin	$1.90	10	$1,900	$50.00	$12,500	15.2%

At first glance, it appears that it would be better to sell naked puts using margin to receive the higher, leveraged return. However, if the trade goes against you and you are forced to purchase stock at $50.00, your broker has to cover the remaining $37,500. You have borrowed this amount and now you find yourself in debt to your broker. Not only will you have to pay back the remaining balance, you will also be charged interest fees on the borrowed amount. When all is said and done, you will have paid more than $50,000 if you had sold the put on margin, whereas the more conservative, cash-secured investor would have paid only the $50,000 obligation.

If you decide to sell naked puts using margin to leverage the position, you must be careful not to overextend your position. You should only sell the number of contracts that equate to the number of shares of stock you could afford to purchase.

For example, if you have $50,000 in funds available you could:

A. Buy 1,000 shares of stock XYZ at $50.00.

B. Sell 10 contracts of the XYZ 50 strike put and be totally cash-secured.

C. Sell 40 contracts of the XYZ 50 strike put on 25 percent margin.

Even though option "C" would yield a leveraged return, selling 40 contracts would obligate the put seller to purchase 4,000 shares of a $50.00 stock. The total risk on the margined position is still $50,000, but the total cash obligation if the shares of XYZ are assigned is $200,000.

NOTE: *Returns throughout this text will be calculated assuming that the investor is totally cash-secured for the sale of the put option.*

BUYING SHARES OF STOCK AT A DISCOUNT

You have researched XYZ, and you have a bullish sentiment on the stock for the next eight months to a year. The stock is currently trading at $56.00 per share, but your target price for purchase is $50.00. Instead of buying 1,000 shares today at $56.00 for a total cost of $56,000, you can sell 10 contracts of the $50 strike put one month out for $0.80. You would collect a premium of $800.00 (premium * # of contracts * 100) against $50,000 (cash-secured funds on hold). If the stock stays above $50.00 in 30 days, the put contract will expire worthless and you will keep the $800.00.

Let's say the put contract does expire worthless after 30 days. The next month out $50 strike put is selling for $0.90. You can repeat the process and sell 10 contracts of the $50 strike put for the next month's expiration for $0.90. You collect another $900.00 against the same $50,000 cash-secured funds. The next 30 days pass and the stock remains above $50.00. Your second sold put expires worthless as did the first put, and you keep the premium.

The Monday following the second month's expiration, you sell a third 50 strike put against XYZ for $0.85. You collect $850.00 against the same $50,000 you started with. At the end of the third expiration period, the stock is trading at $49.00 due to a recent deflation in the market.

Your 10 contracts are *assigned*, meaning you are forced to buy 1,000 shares of XYZ at $50.00 per share though the shares are trading at $49.00. Your broker will use the $50,000 on hold in your account to purchase the assigned shares.

So what? You could not be in a better situation. You did your homework. You know this recent deflation in price is just due to other circumstances in the market not necessarily a weakness in the stock. Your long-term sentiment on XYZ is still bullish. You purchased the 1,000 shares at your target price of $50.00 but your cost basis is much lower than that.

Remember, 10 put contracts were sold three times (table 2.2). The total premium collected was $2.55. In the first month $0.80, per share was collected; in the second month, $0.90; in the third month, $0.85. Those premiums are kept regardless if the option is assigned or if it expires. Even though shares of XYZ were assigned at $50.00 per share, $2.55 per share had been collected during the past three months, making the cost basis only $47.45 per share. The shares of stock were purchased at a greater discounted rate from your initial target price.

Table 2.2 – Rolled 50 Strike Put During Three months

Put Sold (10 Contracts)	Date Sold	Premium Received	Stock Price at Time of Trade	Stock Price at Expiration
March 50	February 20	$0.80	56	54 (Put Expires)
April 50	March 19	$0.90	54	55 (Put Expires)
May 50	April 23	$0.85	55	49 (Assignment)

- Total Premium = $2.55
- Obligation: $50,000 (10 contracts at 50 strike)
- Stock Purchase Price: $50.00
- Cost Basis: $47.45 ($50.00 – $2.55)

Even though the shares were assigned to you at $50.00, your overall cost basis is still below the trading price of the stock, and overall your sentiment is still bullish.

Figure 2.2 – Option Chain

Strike	Put Sym		Opt Bid	Opt Ask	Time Value	% Time Value	% Naked Yield
Infosys Techs. Inc. (INFY) $ 50.00				**JUNE Expiring 6/16/2007 18 days left**			**Hold ☑**
45.00	UNRI		0.10	0.20	0.10	0.2%	0.2%
50.00	UNRJ		1.40	1.55	1.00	2.0%	2.0%
55.00	UNRK		5.50	5.80	0.10	0.2%	0.2%
60.00	UNRL		10.30	10.80	-0.10	-0.2%	-0.1%
65.00	UNRM		15.40	15.70	0.00	0.0%	0.0%
Infosys Techs. Inc. (INFY) $ 50.00				**JULY Expiring 7/21/2007 53 days left**			**Hold ☑**
40.00	UNSH		0.05	0.15	0.05	0.1%	0.1%
45.00	UNSI	OTM Put Bid Price:	0.60	0.70	Time Value: 0.60	1.2%	% Return: 1.3%
50.00	UNSJ		2.30	2.40	2.30	4.6%	4.6%
55.00	UNSK	ITM Put Bid Price:	5.40	6.10	Time Value: 0.40	0.8%	% Return: 0.7%
60.00	UNSL		10.40	10.80	0.00	0.0%	0.0%

Source: PowerOptions (www.poweropt.com)

Understanding of this fundamental philosophy of the naked put strategy helps the investor determine the best strike price to sell. If we look at Figure 2.2, we see that ITM puts (those with a strike price above the current stock price) have a higher bid price.

From this option chain we see that the 55 strike puts for June and July are selling for above $5.00 per contract. In comparison, the 45 strike puts for June and July are selling for below $1.00 per contract. Naked puts are an income-generating strategy. The investor's goal is to sell the put that offers the best return. A common and dangerous misconception by investors just beginning to study options is that the strike that offers the highest premium is the best option to sell.

Figure 2.2 also shows the Percent Naked Yield column. The *percent naked yield* is the potential return for the naked put trade. This return assumes that the position would be cash-secured. From the chain we see that the July 55 strike naked put trade would only yield a 0.7 percent return, where in comparison the July 45 strike put would potentially yield 1.3 percent.

But, how is that possible? The July 55 put could be sold for a premium of $5.40 per share, where the July 45 put only has a premium of $0.60!

In Chapter 1, the concepts of time value and intrinsic value were defined. The July 55 put is 5 points In-the-Money (ITM). When investors sell a put, they are agreeing to buy shares of stock at the strike price. Since the stock is trading at $50.00 per share, an investor that sold the July 55 strike put is agreeing to buy the shares of stock for $5.00 per share *more* than the market price. If the put was assigned and the investor had to buy shares of stock at $55.00, he or she is already losing $5.00. The remaining $0.40 of the $5.40 July 55 premium is time value.

> **Trading Tip:** When an investor sells an option, either a put or a call, the percent naked yield is based on the time value of the option, not the entire premium collected!

The OTM July 45 put is selling for $0.60 per contract. Since this option is OTM, the entire $0.60 is time value as there is no intrinsic value. The investor who sells the 45 put is agreeing to buy shares of stock for five points less than the current market price.

The percent naked yield equals: Time Value (potential profit)/
Put Strike Price (obligation)
The percent naked yield on the July 45 put is:
$0.60/$45 = 1.3%
The percent naked yield on the July 55 put is:
$0.40/$55 = 0.7%

Not only is the time value lower on the ITM put, the total obligation of the contract is higher as well. Regardless of the lower return, selling an ITM put goes against the fundamental concepts of the two kinds of naked put investors. Investors in Group 1 have done their research and are looking to buy shares of stock at a discount. Group 2 investors want the higher premium, but they do not want to be forced to buy shares of stock. The investors of Group 2 are looking for inflated premiums on riskier stocks but they still want the put to expire worthless so they keep the entire premium. Selling the July 55 put would obligate them to buy shares of stock at a higher price than the current market value, the exact opposite concept of their trading methodology.

An investor that sold the July 55 put would need a significant movement in the stock price to have the option expire worthless. If the stock did move up above $55.00, the put would expire worthless, and the investor would keep the entire $5.40; but the odds of that happening are very slim. For the sake of argument, let's say the stock soared up above $70.00 per share during that time frame. The investor would keep the entire premium, but would not take advantage of the swift movement in the underlying stock beyond the $5.40 premium.

> **Trading Tip:** If you were very bullish on a stock and expected a large move over a short period of time, you would earn a higher profit buying a call option or buying the shares of the underlying security. Income-generating strategies, such as naked puts, are designed to help investors profit from a sideways or slightly bullish market. Naked puts are profitable in raging bull markets, but other strategies could be used to increase the returns in those conditions.

You might be asking yourself, "Wait, what about the July 50 put? You did not describe that trade in the previous example, and it shows the highest percent naked yield of 4.6 percent."

Of course, you are right. In this scenario, we simply wanted to illustrate the main point of selling OTM puts versus ITM puts with an example stock that was trading right at a strike price. Rarely can you find stocks that are trading right at a strike price, since stocks are highly liquid vehicles. Now is a good time to break down the three types of investors that trade any strategy. Whether you just invest in mutual funds, bonds, buy and hold strategies on stocks or ETFs, or you are an advanced derivatives investor, you can be referenced as one of three types: conservative, moderate, or aggressive.

THE THREE INVESTMENT APPROACHES

It has been mentioned that there are generally two groups of naked put investors: Those who have researched the stock and are looking to purchase shares at a discount, and those looking for the higher profits on riskier investments. Within each group of naked put investors the three separate divisions of a conservative, moderate, or aggressive investor could be cataloged.

Let's reference back to Figure 2.2, and let's assume that investors of both Group 1 and Group 2 searched out the example stock as the one that matched their investing methodologies.

A conservative investor would look to sell the put that offered a decent premium but still offered a relatively high amount of protection. The conservative naked put investor would sell the 45 strike put that offered a potential 1.3 percent return, an 11.2 percent to break even (protection) with about a 7-in-10 chance of earning the 1.3 percent return.

The trade offers a decent potential return, high protection, and a strong chance of earning the decent return. That's conservative.

A moderate investor is willing to give up some protection in order to gain a higher potential return, but is not looking for the long ball, home run trade. The moderate investor would most likely sell the July 50 put. This has a potential return of 4.6 percent, a 4.6 percent to break even (protection) with about a 50-50 chance of earning the 4.6 percent return.

This trade offers a strong potential return, strong protection, and an average chance of earning the strong return. That's considered to be a moderate trading methodology.

An aggressive investor is simply allured by the potential of a high return and is willing to sacrifice most if not all of the protection to get that return. The aggressive investor would sell the July 55 put. This has a low percent naked yield, but if the stock rose above $55.00 per share, the aggressive investor would keep the entire $5.40 premium. If that happened, the aggressive investor would have a 9.8 percent return (premium/strike price = $5.40/$55), but only a 0.8 percent to break even and about a 1-in-5 chance of getting the 9.8 percent return.

High potential return, no protection, and a slim chance of earning the high return? That is definitely aggressive.

Now you might be asking yourself, "Where did they come up with the 7-in-10 chance of being successful on the conservative trade, the 50-50 chance of the moderate trade, and the 1-in-5 chance for the aggressive trade?"

Probability: There are many parameters that options investors use to evaluate the potential success of a trade being profitable. The most common criteria that investors use is the *percent probability.* This probability reflects the likelihood that a stock will be trading at-or-above or at-or-below a specific strike price at a certain expiration date. This value is determined by looking at the closing price of the stock during the last 52 weeks and taking the standard deviation of those closing prices. Based on that value, we can determine the likelihood that the stock will be trading at, above, or below any given price over any period of time.

To simplify this, there are only two calculations used for any given option:

Percent Probability Above: The theoretical probability that the stock will be trading at or above a specific strike price at the expiration date.

Percent Probability Below: The theoretical probability that the stock will be trading at or below a specific strike price at the expiration date.

Let's refer back to our Option Chain, this time with the Probabilities added in the data columns (Figure 2.3).

Strike	Put Sym	Opt Bid	Opt Ask	Time Value	% Time Value	% Naked Yield	% Break Even	% Prob. Above	% Prob. Below
Figure 2.3 – Option Chain Featuring the Percent Probability Above and Percent Probability Below									
Infosys Techs. Inc. (INFY) $50.00				JUNE Expiring 6/16/2007 18 days left					Hold ☑
45.00	IUNRI	0.10	0.20	0.10	0.2%	0.2%	9.5%	94.6%	5.4%
50.00	IUNRJ	1.40	1.55	1.00	2.0%	2.0%	2.1%	45.0%	55.0%
55.00	IUNRK	5.50	5.80	0.10	0.2%	0.2%	0.2%	5.3%	94.7%
60.00	IUNRL	10.30	10.80	-0.10	-0.2%	-0.1%	-0.3%	0.1%	99.9%
65.00	IUNRM	15.40	15.70	0.00	0.0%	0.0%	0.0%	0.1%	99.9%
Infosys Techs. Inc. (INFY) $50.00				JULY Expiring 7/21/2007 53 days left					Hold ☑
40.00	IUNSH	0.05	0.15	0.05	0.1%	0.1%	19.5%	97.4%	2.6%
45.00	IUNSI	0.60	0.70	0.60	1.2%	1.3%	11.2%	84.1%	15.9%
50.00	IUNSJ	2.30	2.40	2.30	4.6%	4.6%	4.6%	49.7%	50.3%
55.00	IUNSK	5.40	6.10	0.40	0.8%	0.7%	0.8%	17.9%	82.1%
60.00	IUNSL	10.40	10.80	0.00	0.0%	0.0%	0.0%	4.1%	95.9%

Source: PowerOptions (www.poweropt.com)

Theoretically, there are only two extreme values of a probability, 0 percent and 100 percent. If we take a look at the June options, we see that the June 45 put has a 94.6 *percent probability above*, meaning there is a 94.6 percent theoretical chance that the stock will be trading at or above $45.00 per share on June expiration. If a stock has a 94.6 percent theoretical probability that it will be trading above $45.00 on June expiration, then by rule the stock would only have a 5.4 percent *percent probability below*, meaning there is a 5.4 percent theoretical chance that the stock will be trading below $45.00 per share at expiration. If you compare the two probability columns throughout the option chain, you will be able to see that the sum of the two probabilities for any strike price will always equal 100 percent.

Since the objective of the naked put trade is to earn a profit, which occurs when the stock is trading above the put strike price at expiration, our main focus will be on the *percent probability above*. The naked put investor is more focused on the theoretical chance that the stock will be trading above the strike price and having the put expire worthless.

Looking at the available strike prices in the July expiration month, we can assume that the conservative naked put investor would sell the 45 strike put, the moderate naked put investor would sell the ATM 50 strike put, and the really aggressive speculator might look to sell the 55 strike put.

The conservative trade, the July 45 strike put, has a potential 1.3 percent naked yield with an 84.1 percent theoretical probability of earning that return. Remember, a conservative investor is looking to make a decent return, to have a good probability of making that return, and to potentially buy shares of stock at a discount. The July 45 put option would fit that criteria for a conservative naked put investor. Note that the 84.1 percent probability above is greater than the 7-in-10 chance of success we mentioned. Not every optionable stock will have an 84 percent probability above on the 1 strike OTM put. The 7-in-10 chance, or 70 percent probability above we mentioned, is more of an average for puts that are one strike out-of-the-money or more.

A moderate naked put investor might sell the ATM July 50 put. This has a potential 4.5 percent naked yield with a 49.7 percent probability above. I'd say that 49.7 percent probability is about as close to a 50-50 chance as one could get, wouldn't you agree? Most ATM options will have a percent probability above right around 50 percent. This means the stock has a 50-50 chance of moving above its current price by July expiration or dropping below its current price.

The aggressive naked put investor is trying to get the higher premium but has little chance of keeping the entire premium at expiration. The aggressive investor could sell the July 55 put for $5.50 per contract, but he or she would only have a 17.9 percent chance of getting that return. This is an extremely risky position, and we cannot think of any customer we have ever had that tried to sell ITM naked puts. At least, we cannot think of any customers during the last 10 years that were able to sell ITM naked puts and consistently earn a profit. Again, not every put that is one strike ITM will have a 17.9 percent probability above, but can you see our point? High potential reward, high risk, low potential chance of getting the high potential return: These aggressive trades should be avoided at all costs if you are interested in keeping your portfolio value intact.

For the remainder of this text, we will not even discuss the potential of selling ITM naked puts. Selling ITM naked puts goes against the fundamental concepts of this strategy and can lead to large losses.

Our goal is to help you see the advantages of this income-generating strategy and teach you how you can find potential naked put trades that will avoid unnecessary risks. As mentioned before, if you are extremely bullish on a stock, you would be better off researching the long call stock option strategy instead of selling ITM naked puts.

> **Trading Tip:** We have said that when investors sell a naked put, they are obligated to buy shares of stock anytime up to the expiration date of the option. ITM puts have a tendency to be assigned early. Although the ITM seller might receive a high premium, being assigned early can cause a large loss if the stock continues to decline. We will instead show you how to profit and be protected by selling (writing) ATM or OTM naked puts.

Whether you decide to pursue a more conservative methodology for trading naked puts or you decide to be somewhat moderate in your selections, one cannot be successful without an understanding of the various factors that comprise the pricing of a given option.

THE IMPORTANCE OF VOLATILITY

If you are reading this text, you most likely have some trading experience in analyzing stocks, mutual funds, bonds, or some other trading vehicle. Most likely, you have purchased shares of stock in a given industry and watched as it remained in a certain trading range over a period of time while other stocks in that same sector or industry went up, came back down, then maybe shot back up again.

As mentioned before, stocks are highly liquid vehicles. Blue chip stocks, such as IBM and Microsoft, have a tendency to stay in a certain trading range over time. These types of companies have a high average daily volume, a multitude of products and, in some cases, decades of proven success. Because of these attributes, there is a low possibility that these types of stocks would go into bankruptcy or suffer a sharp decline in the underlying price. They are more stable because of their large size and proven track records. This makes them perfect for a *buy and hold* type of investment when planning for retirement, but they are not likely to offer high returns in a short-term investment.

In contrast, companies that have just gone public, biotech companies, and businesses with a highly unstable, hit-or-miss revenue stream, will tend to have wild fluctuations in the underlying stock price over time. Although these lurid types of investments can lead to large profits, they can also cause the investor to suffer major losses and throbbing headaches.

The rate, or tendency, of a stock to fluctuate in price is called *volatility*. Volatility (also called historical volatility) reflects the percentage change in the underlying stock price during the last 52 weeks, calculated by taking one standard deviation of the overall price changes of the security during that one-year span. Although volatility can be calculated using different time frames, the one-year range is the industry standard. It is also the standard used for pricing models, such as the *Black-Scholes* equation.

> **Trading Tip:** You may see different ranges of the volatility measure such as the 20-day, 50-day, 100-day, 200-day, and 250-day. Another way to measure volatility is using the Stocks Implied Volatility Index (SIV). The SIV is the average implied volatility of the near term ITM and OTM calls and puts for a given stock. The SIV measures how the near term options are most likely to react with shifts in the market. Naked put investors will typically sell puts that have less than 45 days to expiration. Therefore, the 50-day volatility and the SIV are the best measures of volatility to use when analyzing a naked put trade.

Using some of the stocks mentioned above, let's compare the different volatilities of those companies (at the time this text was written):

IBM – International Business Machines

52-Week Trading Range – $72.73 to $108.05
Current Price – $106.00
Current Volatility – 0.18 (18%)

MSFT – Microsoft Corp

52-Week Trading Range – $21.46 to $31.48
Current Price – $30.74
Current Volatility – 0.22 (22%)

The volatility for these two companies is fairly low. As a market gauge, the average volatility on all optionable stocks is roughly .30 (30 percent). IBM only has a volatility of 0.18, meaning during the next 52 weeks, IBM will probably be trading within 18 percent of its current price. MSFT has a volatility of 0.22, meaning that it is likely that MSFT will be trading within 22 percent of its current price per share. Many options investors will trade neutral strategies on the indexes such as SPX (S&P 500) or NDX (Nasdaq 100). The price of these securities is based on the myriad of top stocks that comprise that index. Therefore, large changes in the prices of the indexes are highly unlikely unless there is a major market correction. In comparison, the SPX has a volatility of only 0.08 (8 percent) and NDX has a volatility of 0.11 (11 percent).

In contrast, let's look at a biotech company, AtheroGenics Inc. (AGIX), and Odyssey Marine Exploration (OMR), which is a shipwreck salvage company (treasure hunters):

AGIX – AtheroGenics Inc.

52-Week Trading Range – $2.16 to $15.75
Current Price – $2.46
Current Volatility – 2.34 (234%)

OMR – Odyssey Marine Exploration

52-Week Trading Range – $1.52 to $9.45
Current Price – $6.71
Current Volatility – .57 (57%)

These two companies are lower-priced companies and tend to fluctuate in a wider percentage price range. AGIX is subjected to FDA approvals on its line of experimental drugs, whereas the majority of OMR's revenue is based on the value of the coins and artifacts it can salvage from centuries-old shipwrecks. AGIX has a current volatility of 2.34, meaning the stock will most likely be trading within 234 percent of its current price during the next 52 weeks. For OMR, we could expect that the price per share will be 57 percent above or below its current price within the next 52 weeks.

Many investors and stock or option educators will refer to the volatility as "risk." Stocks with a higher volatility will tend to fluctuate in price more often, adding a higher risk that the position will cause a loss, regardless if the investor is bullish or bearish. Volatility is not a bullish or bearish indicator. It is simply a measure of the likelihood that a stock will be trading within a range during the next year based on the performance of the stock during the previous year.

Although past performance is no guarantee of future outcome, it is one of the best gauges investors can use in expectation of future performance. That being said, you might be wondering about the accuracy of volatility.

Using the SmartHistoryXL tool, PowerOptions's back-testing module, we can look back in time and view the past stock price and volatility at that time and compare it to today's current price:

IBM – International Business Machines

> Stock Price on April 28, 2006 - $82.34
> Volatility on April 28, 2006 - 0.13 (13%)
> Stock Price on April 30, 2007 - $102.21
> Volatility on April 30, 2007 - 0.18 (18%)
> **Result:** IBM is trading 24 percent above its price from one year ago.

MSFT – Microsoft Corp.

> Stock Price on April 28, 2006 - $24.15
> Volatility on April 28, 2006 - 0.12 (12%)
> Stock Price on April 30, 2007 - $29.94
> Volatility on April 30, 2007 - 0.22 (22%)
> **Result:** MSFT is trading 24 percent above its price from one year ago.

AGIX – AtheroGenics Inc.

> Stock Price on April 28, 2006 - $14.15
> Volatility on April 28, 2006 - 0.26 (26%)
> Stock Price on April 30, 2007 - $3.35
> Volatility on April 30, 2007 - 2.34 (234%)
> **Result:** AGIX is trading 76 percent below its price from one year ago.

We can see that IBM and Microsoft almost doubled their expected volatilities, where something drastic occurred with the biotech stock. AGIX's underlying price is subject to FDA rulings on its line of potential drugs. The stock had a period of decline during which the price dropped from about $15.00 to the $10.00 range, then came a disastrous ruling on a drug in Phase III trial and the stock plummeted from the $10.00 to the sub $3.00 range. During this time period, the volatility shifted from 0.26 (26 percent) to 0.85 (85 percent) to as high as 2.36 (236 percent) after the large plummet in the stock price.

As with any probability calculation, the longer the time frame, the greater the chance of error. It should also be mentioned that in the months of April to May 2007, the S&P 500, Dow Jones Industrials, and Nasdaq 100 indexes started to hit new record highs.

In addition to reflecting the past performance, the volatility of a stock is used to calculate several other criteria that options investors and naked put sellers use to compare positions. Earlier in this chapter, we discussed the percent probability, the theoretical chance the stock will be trading at or above a certain strike price at the expiration date. The percent probability is derived from the volatility value of a stock. Taking the current price of the stock and the volatility number, we can extrapolate the probability that the stock will be trading above a certain price 30, 45, 60, 90, 120, or 250 days out in time. Without volatility, we could not calculate the probability above criteria mentioned earlier in this chapter.

Volatility is also the main component of the *Black-Scholes Pricing Model*. The Black-Scholes model is very important to any options investor. Fischer Black and Myron Scholes developed the equation in the 1970s, and they were awarded the Nobel Prize for its development. The Black-Scholes Pricing Model calculates the fair market value of an option based on five factors:

1. Underlying stock price
2. Strike price of the option
3. Days remaining to the expiration date
4. Current interest rates
5. *Volatility of the stock*

We do not need to go into the specifics of this equation, but it is important to know the five factors that are used to determine the theoretical worth of the put you are researching. For example, let's say you have found two stocks that you are bullish on and both stocks are trading at $43.00. You are hoping to sell the 40 strike put against either stock A or stock B for the next expiration month. The 40 strike put on stock A has a theoretical value of $1.00 per contract, whereas the 40 strike put on stock B has a theoretical value of $2.10 per contract. How can there be such a wide discrepancy between the theoretical values of these two similar options?

The answer: Volatility. Let's look at the five factors again:

1. Underlying stock price – Both stock A and B are trading at $43.00.
2. Strike price of the option – Both are 40 strike puts.
3. Days remaining to the expiration date – Both puts are one month out.
4. Current interest rates – Constant across the entire market.
5. *Volatility*—Aha! As we learned, volatility is different depending on the price history of the stock.

In this example, we could assume that stock A had been trading in a relatively tight range during the last 52 weeks, whereas stock B might have had several price fluctuations due to bad or good earnings, successful or unsuccessful new product lines, or potentially even a boardroom scandal. Because stock B has fluctuated in price so much, it has a higher risk of dropping suddenly below the strike price of the put option. One of the standard rules of any investing strategy is that with higher risk comes a higher potential reward. Stock B is a riskier investment that might have a history of sudden price fluctuations; therefore, the option premiums are inflated due to the added risk. This is why the theoretical value of the 40 strike put for stock B is so much higher then the 40 strike put for stock A, even though the two securities are trading at the same price.

There are two other things you need to know regarding the Black-Scholes Pricing Model and the option's theoretical worth. First, the Black-Scholes Pricing Model was developed based on *European-style* options. European-style options can only be assigned or exercised on the option's expiration date. *American style* options can be exercised or assigned anytime between the day the option is sold until the expiration date. This is one of the reasons why put or call options can be bought or sold at values that are slightly different from their theoretical worth. Second, even though you may hear some investors say that the Black-Scholes model is not an accurate model to evaluate the price of an option, it is the most-used model by brokers, knowledgeable investors, data sources, and even market makers who set the actual trading prices of the listed options.

If you look at a given option chain or if you are using a Black-Scholes calculator, you know that very rarely, if ever, will an option be trading at the same price as its theoretical worth. For example, if the 40 strike put on stock A had a theoretical worth of $1.00, it might be trading on the market for $1.50. What would cause such a high percentage difference in the actual trading price of the option and it's theoretical worth? The answer: *implied volatility.*

Implied volatility is the value that justifies the actual trading price of the option. Another way to define implied volatility of an option is to say that the implied volatility of an option reflects the overall future expectation of the volatility of the underlying stock.

The implied volatility of an option is better understood by taking a look at how it is calculated.

Remember, the Black-Scholes Pricing Model takes into account five factors to determine an options theoretical worth:

Stock price
Strike price
Days to expiration   **Theoretical option value**
Current interest rates
Volatility

However, we know that the actual trading price of the option is usually different than its theoretical worth. If we replace the answer of the equation, the theoretical Black-Scholes value, and replace that value with the actual trading price of the option and remove the volatility variable, we have:

Stock price
Strike price
Days to expiration   **Actual option price**
Current interest rates
Variable X

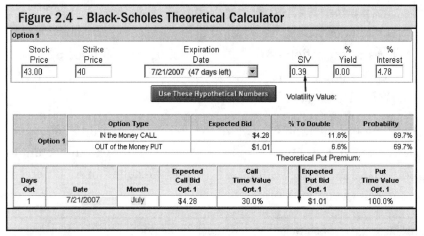

Figure 2.4 – Black-Scholes Theoretical Calculator

Option 1

	Stock Price	Strike Price	Expiration Date		SIV	% Yield	% Interest
	43.00	40	7/21/2007 (47 days left) ▼		0.39	0.00	4.78

Use These Hypothetical Numbers   Volatility Value:

	Option Type	Expected Bid	% To Double	Probability
Option 1	IN the Money CALL	$4.28	11.8%	69.7%
	OUT of the Money PUT	$1.01	6.6%	69.7%

Theoretical Put Premium:

Days Out	Date	Month	Expected Call Bid Opt. 1	Call Time Value Opt. 1	Expected Put Bid Opt. 1	Put Time Value Opt. 1
1	7/21/2007	July	$4.28	30.0%	$1.01	100.0%

Source: PowerOptions (www.poweropt.com)

When we work the equation backward to solve for Variable X, the removed volatility, we are solving for the implied volatility that justifies the actual trading price of the option. Let's take our example and use the PowerOptions Black-Scholes calculator to better reflect this concept (Figure 2.4).

Stock price - $43.00
Strike price - $40
Days to expiration - 47   } **Theoretical put value of $1.01**
Current interest rates - 4.78%
Volatility - 0.39 (39%)

Initially, the volatility of the stock is equal to 0.39, or 39 percent. This gives us an expected put value of $1.01. Now we can enter a value to find what volatility value would justify the price of the option as it is actually trading for $1.50 (the implied volatility). Here we see that a volatility value of 0.48, or 48 percent would justify the option price of $1.50:

Stock price - $43.00

Strike price - $40

Days to expiration - 47   **Actual trading price $1.51.**

Current interest rates - 4.78%

[Volatility Variable X]

Working the equation backward, we find that a volatility of 0.48 (48 percent) would give us a calculated value of $1.51. It is important to note that a 20 percent change in volatility resulted in a 50 percent change in the option's price.

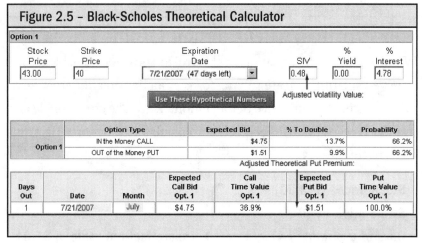

Figure 2.5 – Black-Scholes Theoretical Calculator

In our example, the historical volatility of the stock was 0.39 (39 percent), which gave us a theoretical worth of about $1.00. Using the PowerOptions Black-Scholes Calculator, we see that the implied volatility of the option would be around 0.48 (48 percent) to justify the actual trading price of the option.

A term we commonly use to describe implied volatility is "double-edged sword." As put writers, our goal is to find the option with the best percent naked yield ... but at the same time we want a strong probability of earning that percentage without any potential surprises. Put options with a high implied volatility do offer a more inflated premium but there is a larger possibility the stock could swing wildly and cause a large loss. The option premium is inflated for some future reason: upcoming earnings, completion of a large product line or project, FDA approval (in the case of a biotech company), and pending lawsuits or some other potential court proceeding. These events, over which management has no control, could cause a sudden and substantial increase or decrease in the underlying stock price. As stated before, the put that offers the highest premium is not always the best trade.

> **Trading Tip:** We could spend chapters and chapters of text describing the volatility equation, the percentages of the standard deviation curve and how those ranges are used to determine the probability and volatility. For the purposes of this text, it is important to illustrate the concept that volatile stocks and options on those stocks are riskier investments. If you wanted to do further research on volatility and how it relates to options pricing, we highly recommend Sheldon Natenberg's *Option Volatility Trading Strategies*.

Having knowledge of the Black-Scholes pricing model, historical volatility, and implied volatility can help you avoid selling undervalued put options while at the same time help you avoid put trades that might have unnecessary risk due to an upcoming event.

LIQUIDITY

Another important criteria that naked put investors should examine is the *liquidity* of the option they are hoping to sell. The liquidity refers to the trading activity of the option, measured by daily *volume* (how many contracts have been traded on a given day) and the *open interest* (the number of open option contracts on the market over the life of the contract).

Options with a low daily volume and a low open interest typically will have a wider bid-ask spread. When investors sell a naked put, they need to be aware of the potential risks of the trade. If the underlying security drops below the strike price of the sold put, the investor will have to buy shares of stock, or the investor can buy to close the option, canceling the obligation of the contract. If the put option has a wide bid-ask spread due to low interest, the investor may lose a significant percentage of expected profit if they have to close the option prior to the expiration date. On a side note, put options with a higher implied volatility or put options with a large spike in volume might also have a wide bid-ask spread.

As a general rule, investors should make sure the option has some volume and open interest on the day they are looking to place the trade. To be more conservative, we suggest screening for a put option where the current volume is five times the number of contracts you are planning to sell, and the open interest is 10 times the number of contracts you are going to trade. If we were looking to sell five contracts, we would want the current volume to be at least 25 or more and the open interest to be at least 50; for a 10 contract trade, we would want to see a minimum current volume of 50 contracts with an open interest greater than 100 contracts.

This ratio is important, as an investor does not want to be the entire market. If one was going to sell 10 contracts and the current volume was zero and the open interest was two, the investor is setting the majority of the interest for that put option. He or she may not be able to receive the best premium if a simple market order was placed since there is little interest on the position. Investors may also have some difficulty closing the trade if the stock moved against them due to a lack of liquidity. If investors set the market by trading the largest block of contracts, they are essentially trading against the market maker, which could lead to undesirable trading results.

THE GREEKS: MONITORING THE MOVEMENT OF THE OPTION

Once you have entered into a naked put trade, you need to monitor the price changes of the option that you sold. The various tools and some rules of thumb for monitoring and managing the position will be discussed in Chapter 6. When entering the trade, there are certain criteria that can be used to gauge how the option will potentially change in price as the stock moves in price and as the position nears the expiration date. The two most significant criteria are the *delta* and the *theta*.

Delta is the value that one should expect the option premium to change in relation to a one-point movement in the underlying stock price. For example, a call option with a delta of 0.50 will theoretically gain $0.50 in value if the underlying stock gains $1.00. Call options are bullish investment vehicles and gain in value when the stock price increases; therefore, call options have a positive delta.

Put options are bearish investment vehicles and will decrease in value as the stock price rises. This means that put options have a negative delta in relation to one point upward movement in the underlying stock price. A put option with a delta of −0.50 will theoretically lose $0.50 in value if the underlying stock gains $1.00. Conversely, if the stock dropped $1.00 in value the put option would theoretically gain $0.50.

At-the-Money options will typically have a delta of .50 for call options and −.50 for put options. Deep in-the-money calls will have a delta value closer to 1. A call option with a delta of 1 will gain in value equal to the increase in the underlying security. Deep in-the-money puts will have a delta value closer to −1, meaning that the put option will decline in value equal to the increase in the price of the stock and gain in value equal to a decline in the stock price. Deeper out-of-the-money calls and puts will have a delta closer to zero.

Figure 2.6 shows a partial call and put chain with the delta values selected in the results field.

In this example, the stock is trading at $52.45. Note the deep in-the-money August 40 strike call is currently selling for $12.60 and has a delta of 1. If the stock gained one point in value, we would also expect the premium of the call to go up one point to a new premium of $13.60.

Figure 2.6 – Partial Call and Put Chain Featuring Delta Criteria

Strike	Call Sym	Opt Bid	% In Money	Delta	Put Sym	Opt Bid	% In Money	Delta
Infosys Techs. Inc. (INFY) $ 50.00			AUGUST Expiring 8/18/2007 31 days left					Hold ☑
40.00 IJNHH	12.60		24.0%	ITM Call:1.00	IJNTH	0.00	-24.0%	-
45.00 IJNHI	7.80		14.5%	0.99	IJNTI	0.05	-14.5%	-0.01
50.00 IJNHJ	3.30		5.0%	0.78	IJNTJ	0.55	-5.0%	-0.24
55.00 IJNHK	0.80		-4.5%	0.31	IJNTK	2.85	4.5%	-0.69
60.00 IJNHL	0.15		-14.0%	0.05	IJNTL	7.30	14.0%	ITM Put:-0.94
Infosys Techs. Inc. (INFY) $ 50.00			OCTOBER Expiring 10/20/2007 94 days left					Hold ☑
35.00 IJNJG	17.90		33.5%	1.00	IJNVG	0.05	-33.5%	0.00
40.00 IJNJH	13.20		24.0%	0.99	IJNVH	0.20	-24.0%	-0.01
45.00 IJNJI	8.80		14.5%	0.91	IJNVI	0.70	-14.5%	-0.09
50.00 IJNJJ	5.10		5.0%	0.71	IJNVJ	1.90	-5.0%	-0.31
55.00 IJNJK	2.55		-4.5%	0.43	IJNVK	4.30	4.5%	-0.57
60.00 IJNJL	1.10		-14.0%	0.20	IJNVL	7.80	14.0%	-0.80

Source: PowerOptions (www.poweropt.com)

The deep ITM August 60 strike put is currently selling for $7.30 and has a delta of −0.94. If the stock gained one point, we would expect to have the put premium drop $0.94 in value to $6.36. If the stock dropped one point in value, the 60 strike put would theoretically gain $0.94, making the new premium about $8.24.

A naked put investor would potentially look to sell the OTM August 50 put or the August 45 put. The August 45 put has a minimal premium of only $0.05 per contract, which might not cover the transaction cost if the investor was only planning to sell three or four contracts. The August 50 put has a more viable premium of $0.55 and a delta of −0.24. If an investor sold this put option, the investor could expect the option premium to drop $0.24 if the stock gained $1.00, but he or she would also want to be aware that the put option could gain $0.24 in value if the stock dropped $1.00 in value.

If there was a sudden upward move and the option dropped $0.24 in value, the naked put investor could buy to close the contract for about $0.30. The investor would not keep the entire premium, but they would be able to lock in 45 percent of their expected gains in a short period of time. Conversely, if the stock dropped suddenly the premium might gain $0.24 in value causing a 45 percent loss on the position if the investor attempted to buy to close the put before the stock dropped any further. It is important to be aware of the delta in order to be prepared for shifts in the option premium, whether those shifts are in the investor's favor or affect the position negatively.

The next Greek value we want to discuss is *theta*.

Theta measures the rate the option loses value as time passes. Theta is expressed as a negative value because it shows the rate of decline for an option. Theta benefits the option seller and hinders an option buyer.

Theta is not a linear value, as an option will lose a higher percentage of its time value as it gets closer to the expiration date. Figure 2.7 shows the option chain with theta and time value selected.

The August 50 strike put has a time value of $0.35 and 30 days remaining to expiration. If we used a linear equation to calculate theta, we would divide the time value by the days remaining to expiration:

$$\$0.35 \text{ Time Value} / 30 \text{ Days to Expiration} = 0.0116$$
$$\text{(which would be expressed as } -0.0116\text{)}$$

Using this equation, we would expect the value of the option to decline $0.0116 every day through expiration, assuming no change in the underlying stock price or the historical volatility.

From Figure 2.7 we see that the **actual** theta of the August 50 strike put is −0.0147. This means we would expect the option to lose $0.0147 today, and the theta would be recalculated to reflect how much the option would decay for the next day. Theta will adjust over the life of the option as the stock price, volatility, and time value change. As a naked put investor, it is important to use theta to gauge the rate of decline of your sold contract.

The remaining Greeks can also be useful in analyzing a position, but are not as important as delta and theta.

Gamma is the rate the delta changes as the price of the underlying security changes. In our example, the August 50 strike put had a delta of −0.24. If the stock dropped one point, we would expect the put premium to gain $0.24. If the stock gained one point, we would expect the put premium to drop $0.24. Once the stock moved up in price, the delta would adjust as well. If the August 50 strike put had

Figure 2.7 – Partial Call and Put Chain Featuring Theta and Time Value

Strike	Call Sym	Opt Bid	Theta	Time Value	Put Sym	Opt Bid	Theta	Time Value
Infosys Techs. Inc. (INFY) $ 52.65			AUGUST Expiring 8/18/2007 30 days left				Hold ☑	
40.00	IUNHH	12.60	-0.0054	-0.05	IUNTH	Days to Exp: 0.00	-	-
45.00	IUNHI	7.80	-0.0083	0.15	IUNTI	0.05	-0.0022	0.05
50.00	IUNHJ	3.30	-0.0238	0.65	IUNTJ	Premium: 0.35	Theta: -0.0147 (Time Decay)	0.35
55.00	IUNHK	0.80	-0.0246	0.80	IUNTK	2.65	-0.0172	0.50
60.00	IUNHL	0.15	-0.0068	0.15	IUNTL	7.20	0.0013	-0.15
Infosys Techs. Inc. (INFY) $ 52.65			OCTOBER Expiring 10/20/2007 94 days left				Hold ☑	
35.00	IUNJG	17.90	-0.0047	0.25	IUNVG	0.05	-0.0001	0.05
40.00	IUNJH	13.20	-0.0064	0.55	IUNVH	0.20	-0.0010	0.20
45.00	IUNJI	8.80	-0.0111	1.15	IUNVI	0.70	-0.0051	0.70
50.00	IUNJJ	5.10	-0.0169	2.45	IUNVJ	1.90	-0.0102	1.90
55.00	IUNJK	2.55	-0.0171	2.55	IUNVK	4.30	-0.0098	1.95
60.00	IUNJL	1.10	-0.0116	1.10	IUNVL	7.80	-0.0035	0.45

Source: PowerOptions (www.poweropt.com)

a gamma of 0.02, the new delta would be −0.26 (if the stock dropped one point) or −0.22 (if the stock moved up one point).

Vega measures the value that the Black-Scholes number (the theoretical worth of the option) will change due to a change in volatility. This value can give the investor a gauge of how sensitive the option price is in relation to shifts in volatility.

Rho measures the sensitivity of an option's price to a change in interest rates. Call options will generally increase in value when the interest rate increases, whereas put options will decrease in value. Rho has a larger effect on options that are further out in time.

Beta is a stock indicator. Beta measures the underlying security's price sensitivity to changes in the market. The beta of the S&P 500 is one. A stock with a beta less than one would rise and fall in value more slowly than the S&P 500, where a stock with a beta greater than 1 will be more volatile than the S&P 500.

These Greek values can help the investor gauge the movement of the option price or the underlying security, but they are not as important as delta and theta when entering a naked put trade.

Chapter 3

SELECTING THE RIGHT STOCKS

THE NAKED PUT STRATEGY IS A NEUTRAL to bullish strategy; therefore, it is essential to focus your attention on stocks that meet the same criteria. We want to write puts on stocks that hold the same price or go up in price during the write period. The ideal case is to write the put and have it expire worthless because the stock went up in price. Even though we try to write puts on stocks we expect to go up, there will be times when we are wrong for any number of reasons. If a stock gets put to us because it went in-the-money (ITM), it should be one that we would not mind owning for the long term. We may have been wrong in the short term, but we should expect to be right in the longer-term. If the expectations of the company have changed and we are no longer bullish on it, we should not be writing puts on it and should move on to another opportunity. If the expectations change while we have the naked put, we should consider liquidating the position and buy to close the put once it goes ITM. So how do we determine what stocks will be going up?

DETERMINING BULLISH STOCKS

There are many criteria used to determine what stocks will go up in price. Most stock pickers use both fundamental and technical criteria in their evaluations. By *fundamentally* we mean how a company is performing using financial measurements like earnings, cash flow, and sales. And *technically* we mean how its stock price is actually performing. As an example, one might determine if the stock is in an uptrend or at a resistance point or perhaps hitting new highs. *Technical analysis* primarily deals with the chart pattern of the underlying stock. There are some analysts who believe that the fundamentals are already built into the price of the stock and concentrate exclusively on the chart pattern of the stock, while many fundamentalists consider the use of charts paramount to use of voodooism. In reality, both techniques should be used because so many people in each camp follow them. Each makes a contribution to our understanding of what a good company is for our naked put strategy.

What Do the Charts Tell Us?

Technically, we are looking for a stock that has a rising chart pattern. To discern this trend, we generally use a chart program to plot the stock prices during some period of time. Since our put writing is only one or two months out, it is best to use a chart that covers the recent past or about six months out in time. The charts below show a stock in an uptrend (Figure 3.1) and the contrasting down trend (Figure 3.2). Just by looking at the chart you can get a good feel about the trend in stock price with time. These charts are over a five-to-six month period and clearly show the top chart is in an uptrend and the bottom chart is in a downtrend. Figure 3.1 shows uptrend stock prices that are above the 50-day moving average most of the time, which would be favorable for a naked put investment program.

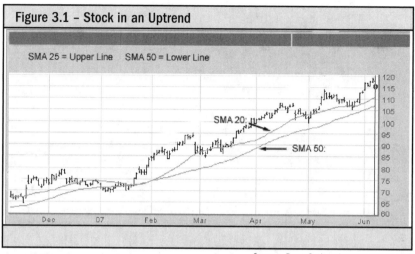

Figure 3.1 – Stock in an Uptrend

SMA 25 = Upper Line   SMA 50 = Lower Line

SMA 20:

SMA 50:

Source: PowerOptions (www.poweropt.com)

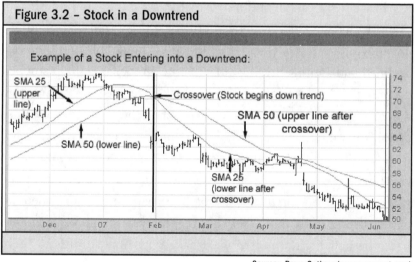

Figure 3.2 – Stock in a Downtrend

Example of a Stock Entering into a Downtrend:

SMA 25 (upper line)

Crossover (Stock begins down trend)

SMA 50 (upper line after crossover)

SMA 50 (lower line)

SMA 25 (lower line after crossover)

Source: PowerOptions (www.poweropt.com)

We actually look for an uptrend for the stock overall but like to sell the put on a downward reaction in the price while in the uptrend. An example of the pattern that is preferred is the one shown in Figure 3.3.

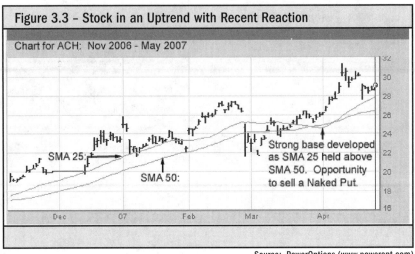

Figure 3.3 – Stock in an Uptrend with Recent Reaction

Chart for ACH: Nov 2006 - May 2007

SMA 25:

SMA 50:

Strong base developed as SMA 25 held above SMA 50. Opportunity to sell a Naked Put.

Dec   07   Feb   Mar   Apr

Source: PowerOptions (www.poweropt.com)

ACH is clearly in an uptrend over the six-month period shown. The price of the stock is above both the 25-day (SMA 25) and 50-day moving averages, which are plotted on the graph. As the price declined and approached the SMA 25 line on the far right, it stopped declining and held its ground. The stock developed a base and presented a great opportunity to sell our put. When the stock declines like this in an overall uptrend, the premium on the put will increase with the slight reaction in the stock. We expect to get a little more value in our put with the slight stock decline and then hopefully the stock will continue on its upward path. Situations like this where we have a strong stock that is moving up and have some retrenchment from the new high are often ideal naked put opportunities. There were several opportunities along the way to write the put. In the one case, where the 25-day and 50-day moving average were both penetrated, it was too risky. It turned out that the stock did hit new highs, in about six weeks, and the put sale would have been fine, but an investment at that time would have been safe only with 20-20 hindsight or a crystal ball.

What Do Fundamentals Tell Us?

Good management is often cited as a prerequisite for a good company, but how do you identify good management? If a manager has a long track record and many years of experience in the company, we can see how the company has performed and attribute the amount of success or failure to that manager. However, managers often change frequently and move from company to company, making it more difficult to tell how they will do in our company. Institutional investors, like the manager of a mutual fund, will often visit a firm they expect to invest in to assess the company. But honestly, do you expect the company to own up to problems? The company will be putting its best foot forward and telling the mutual fund manager what he or she wants to hear. Our only real way to know the quality of management is in the results the company has achieved.

Most important in evaluating a company's performance is its sales growth. Everything comes from sales growth. Even if the company is not yet profitable, with strong sales growth expenses can be cut, operating efficiencies can be improved, and direct costs can be reduced. But without good sales growth, a company is always on the defensive. Their cost of goods and expenses will be under constant pressure, and growing earnings will be very hard to achieve. Even if expenses can be reduced, there is always a limit to decreasing expenses to improve earnings if the sales are not there also. Therefore, look to top line sales growth of at least 15 to 20 percent.

Companies are generally valued by their ability to generate earnings. The sales growth should improve earnings at an increasing rate. As sales grow, the earnings increases should be easier and easier to achieve. One of the measures investors look at is a stocks-price-to-earnings ratio. Therefore, as the earning increase, we would expect the price to move up also. In fact, if the earnings growth is rapid enough, the price-to-earning ratio may increase because the company will be perceived as outperforming. This can often increase the price of the stock very rapidly because it will be driven not only by the earning growth but also by the price-earning ratio. Look for a string of increased earnings during the last few years and, most important, increases over the last few quarters. Earnings should increase at least as fast as sales or faster. In general, if you want to earn 20 percent a year from your investments, then the earnings of your holdings must grow at that rate or greater to succeed in the long run. It is just unreasonable to expect your stock to go up if it is not supported by strong earnings growth.

William O'Neil of *Investors Business Daily* likes companies that have something new in their outlook. Consider favorably a company with a new product, new management or a new high in the price of the stock—something that will bring positive attention to the stock and help drive its price per share higher. This added attention could cause brokers to increase their recommendations on the stock and encourage institutions like mutual funds to increase their purchase of the stock. Both of these effects will help move the stock up in price. Institutions are a major source of volume in today's market. Increases in volume are indicative of institutional activity. This high-volume activity with increasing prices will attract more institutions and often start a buying frenzy. Again you are looking for events that will help move the price of the stock in a positive direction.

It is also good to be in stocks that are favored by the institutions. Certain groups or sectors are favored at different times in the market cycle, while others may fall out of favor. While oil prices are going up, oil, gas, and drilling companies will be very hot, but airlines and trucking may not be so popular because their costs are going up with the price of fuel. It is just easier for your stock to go up if it is in a popular industry. But even more important than the group the stock is in is the overall market environment. Generally, three quarters of any upward movement in stock price comes from the overall market. Everything tends to move together. It is much more difficult for your stock to go up when the overall market is declining. Therefore, try to do your put selling when the market is strong and trending upward. Use a general index like the S&P 500 as a broad gauge on the health of the market. As an example, if the S&P 500 is above its 50-day moving average, the market is probably in an uptrend and your stock of interest will be in an uptrend. The trend is your friend, so keep it positive.

WHAT CAN GO WRONG?

Can we now guarantee that our stock selected from the above steps will not go down? Absolutely not! No matter how careful we are, there will be some cases when the stock falls. In fact, we can be absolutely sure that our puts will at some time get assigned. What we have achieved with our careful choices and research is a higher probability of success; but, we have not guaranteed it.

We owned shares in a health care stock that was a leader in the industry. It had a great earnings record, and the stock price had been moving up to the right for many months. How could it go wrong? Well, it went wrong. In the next month, this stock declined by more than 10 percent because the company was in the process of being audited by the SEC for backdating insider company stock option awards. An event like this had nothing to do with the company's financials or earnings. It had nothing to do with the company's competitive position in the industry or with future industry prospects. But the stock went down on the potential threat of an audit. In this case, we actually looked at the decline in stock price as an opportunity to buy. Therefore, when the stock declined and our naked put went in-the-money (ITM), we let it get assigned to us. And we went one step further and purchased (some) more stock and wrote covered calls on the combined batch of stock. We will discuss recovery from a stock decline in later chapters, but we wanted to emphasize that things do not always go as planned. Although in this case, the stock eventually returned to its previous price and we were very well rewarded for taking advantage of this short-term dislocation in the market.

TECHNOLOGY AS A COMPETITIVE EDGE

Finding the best naked put investments can be a daunting job. It could take many hours in the library, visits to companies, or work on the Internet to find some good prospects. But we do not all have the time and energy necessary to do the research. Just how practical is it to investigate all of these criteria to find a good stock? The process of doing the necessary research to seek out the best companies can be accomplished in another way. Consider using an Internet interactive screening tool to search for your investment opportunities. One such tool is the SmartSearchXL tool provided at http://www. PowerOpt.com.

The SmartSearchXL Tool

This tool will allow an investor to search the entire universe of optionable stocks and all of their 275,000 plus options to find the ones that meet a certain criteria. The search criteria can be a variety of parameters such as earnings growth, capitalization, Z score, broker recommendations, or if the stock is in an uptrend. Fundamental financial parameters, technical chart information, and industry group or market trends can be all monitored and searched simultaneously. Research that once took hours in the library can be reduced to several clicks and a few minutes with a powerful tool like this. Someone not on Wall Street can now reduce what was once a full-time job to a part-time activity. An example naked put screen is shown in Figure 3.4.

Figure 3.4 – SmartSearchXL Tool

Top 4 of 4 results for Naked Put search on May 11, 2007 ordered by % Naked Yield   See More/Less Columns

More Info	Company Name	Stock Sym	Last Stock Price & Chg	Option Sym	Expire/Strike & Days To Exp	Opt Bid	% Naked Yield	% Naked Yield Annual	% Time Value	% Break Even	% In Money	% Prob. Above	Implied Volat.	Volat
▶	MEMC Electronic Materials Inc.	WFR	60.87 (+0.73)	WFRSK	07 JUL 55.0 (71)	2.00	3.6	18.7	3.29	12.9	-9.6	71.5	0.45	0.57
▶	MEMC Electronic Materials Inc.	WFR	60.87 (+0.73)	WFRRK	07 JUN 55.0 (36)	1.00	1.8	18.4	1.64	11.3	-9.6	78.7	0.44	0.57
▶	Manitowoc Company Inc.	MTW	76.50 (+1.57)	MTWRN	07 JUN 70.0 (36)	0.95	1.4	13.8	1.24	9.7	-8.5	79.8	0.37	0.30
▶	Baker Hughes Inc.	BHI	80.37 (+1.52)	BHIRO	07 JUN 75.0 (36)	0.90	1.2	12.2	1.12	7.8	-6.7	78.3	0.31	0.26

☐ Expired

Naked Put search filters   Save   Clear These Settings   Submit These Settings

Sort Results Table By		Greater Than	Less Than		Greater Than	Less Than
% Naked Yield ▼	% Naked Yield	1.0	to 30	% EPS Growth	15	to
Option Expiration Time Frame						
All Months ▼	% Naked Yield Annual	12	to	Price/Earnings	0	to 80
Days To Expiration	% Break Even		to	Price/Earnings/Growth		to
5 to 75	% Break Even Annual		to	% Of 52 Week Range		to
⦿ Order results HIGHEST to LOWEST	Option Volume Today	0	to	Average Broker Rec		to 2.6
○ Order results LOWEST to HIGHEST	% Current Option Volume		to	Average Rec Change		to
Show in-the-money	Prev Option Volume		to	% Stock Volume		to
# Strikes [ ] to [ ]	% Prev Option Volume		to	Shares Outstanding		to
% in money [ ] to [ ]	Open Interest	10	to	% Dividend Yield		to

The tool scans the entire universe of options looking for naked puts that are:

- 8% OTM—This will provide us with at least 8 percent downside protection before our premium is considered. Our break-even point will be this 8 percent plus the premium received on writing the put. This parameter is further down the page and is not show in the above table.

- Naked yields greater than 1.0%—This will assure that we make at least 12 percent per year if we can do 12 writes during the year. There is also an upper limit of 30 percent. This higher limit was intended to screen out the very high risk (high return) biotech issues, which often have unrealistic expectations.

- Option volume greater than 0—We want to be sure there is enough liquidity in the market for our trades. If there is at least one option contract being traded, we have verified some minimum activity. However, trading more than 20 contracts may require moving this value up to 100 or more to provide an activity level that is not dominated by our trades. This parameter is not shown in the results table, but could have been displayed. It was not included to keep the output simple for illustration.

- Open interest greater than 10—This is another measure of liquidity in the market. A general rule is to have the open interest at least 10 times the number of contracts we want to trade. In this case, we are expecting to trade about two contracts. This parameter is not shown in the output table for simplicity.

- Earning growth of greater than 15%—Remember we wanted to be sure the company was growing its earning at about the rate of return we were seeking or higher.

- Broker recommendation less than 2.6 (1 is best)—This setting is looking for brokers, in general, to look at this stock in a favorable light. The lower the number the better the rating. This parameter is not show in the results above to keep the output simple.

- Stocks greater than 50-day moving average (MA) (box not shown)—We used the 50-day moving average relative to the stock price as a means to assure that the stock was in an uptrend. Other moving averages could have been used, but this one was chosen to best match our trading time period. A 20-day MA would have been too short and the 100 would have been too long.

- Stock prices between $5.00 and $100.00—Since we need to secure the naked put with cash in case the option is assigned, the price of the stock can be used to limit the cash needed to be set aside or kept in reserve. If we traded 200 shares (two option contracts) on a stock selling at 100, we would need $20,000 to cover (cash-secured) an assignment of those shares to us if the naked put went ITM.

There were three companies and four options that met those requirements. This search took just a few seconds to scan for stock prices, fundamentals, technical trends, and option returns all at the same time. The "more info" key next to each stock selection is available to provide access to additional information about each of the stock selections presented in a report. A "more info" key is basically a one-stop shop for everything you would need to know about a company (Figure 3.5).

In this case, for the US Steel Group, clicking on the "more info" button produces a list other information specifically about this company:

- BrokerLink—Provides access to the order page of a broker if you want to place that trade. We will discuss this feature in more depth later in the book.

Figure 3.5 – More Information Links From SmartSearchXL

More Info	Company Name	Stock Sym	Last Stock Price & Chg	Option Sym	Expire/Strike & Days To Exp	Opt Bid	% Naked Yield	% Naked Yield Annual	% Time Value	% Break Even	% In Money	% Prob. Above	Implied Volat.	Volat
▶	Microstrategy Inc.	MSTR	102.35 (-7.21)	EOUXP	07 DEC 80.0 (44)	0.75	0.9	7.8	0.7	22.6	-21.84	90.9	0.57	0.48
▶	NYSE Group Inc.	NYX	89.35 (+1.53)	NYXXN	07 DEC 70.0 (44)	0.45	0.6	5.3	0.5	22.2	-21.68	96.7	0.51	0.31
▶	Allegheny Techs. Inc.	ATI	93.04 (-1.72)	ATIXO	07 DEC 75.0 (44)	1.00	1.3	11.1	1.1	20.5	-19.39	88.5	0.56	0.48
▶	Monsanto Co.	MON	98.64 (+4.08)	MONXP	07 DEC 80.0 (44)	0.60	0.8	6.2	0.6	19.5	-18.9	92.4	0.47	0.32
▶	U.S. Steel Group	X	97.44 (-1.42)	XXP	07 DEC 80.0 (44)	1.30	1.6	13.5	1.3	19.2	-17.9	87.2	0.57	0.48
▶	**U.S. Steel Group**	R	102.35 (-7.21)	EOUXQ	07 DEC 85.0 (44)	1.35	1.6	13.2	1.3	18.3	-16.95	84.3	0.55	0.48
▶	BrokerLink ▶		90.23 (+6.54)	MBTXO	07 DEC 75.0 (44)	0.70	0.9	7.7	0.8	17.7	-16.88	84.6	0.55	0.47
▶	Stock Chart ▶		89.40 (-1.04)	MGMXO	07 DEC 75.0 (44)	1.00	1.3	11.1	1.1	17.2	-16.11	89.3	0.50	0.27
▶	Company Info ▶		89.35 (+1.53)	NYXXO	07 DEC 75.0 (44)	0.80	1.1	8.8	0.9	17.0	-16.06	90.6	0.46	0.31
▶	Option Chain ▶		111.38 (+2.50)	LVSXS	07 DEC 95.0 (44)	2.45	2.6	21.4	2.2	16.9	-14.71	77.8	0.59	0.59
▶	Research ▶		94.50 (+1.63)	PRUXP	07 DEC 80.0 (44)	1.10	1.4	11.4	1.2	16.5	-15.34	90.1	0.48	0.26
▶	Calculators ▶		94.41 (-0.26)	SPGXP	07 DEC 80.0 (44)	1.10	1.4	11.4	1.2	16.4	-15.26	88.0	0.48	0.33
▶	Add to Portfolio		93.04 (-1.72)	ATIXP	07 DEC 80.0 (44)	1.75	2.2	18.1	1.9	15.9	-14.02	80.0	0.54	0.48
▶	Profit/Loss Chart		97.44 (-1.42)	XXQ	07 DEC 85.0 (44)	2.20	2.6	21.5	2.3	15.0	-12.77	78.4	0.55	0.46
▶			97.86 (+0.08)	CAMXQ	07 DEC 85.0 (44)	1.40	1.6	13.7	1.4	14.6	-13.14	81.1	0.47	0.38

Source: PowerOptions (www.poweropt.com)

- Stock Chart—Displays a customizable chart similar to the ones shown above.

- Company Info—Provides information on company-specific news, earnings, and events like splits or dividends, and a company profile, which highlights the company's business with financials.

- Option Chain—To display the other strike prices and months of options available for this stock.

- Research—Provides a display of fundamental and technical data for both the stock and this option.

- Calculators—Allows one to calculate the returns, which may include commissions or other costs, and access to a Black-Scholes model for calculating the theoretical value of an option.

- Add to Portfolio—Allows easy insertion of the information to track your stock and option position over time until expiration of the option.

- Profit/Loss Chart—A graphic of this issue's option and stock price on a profit/loss chart.

The concept of this "more info" button was to provide one- or two-click access to all information about any particular company to be used in an option strategy. It is a convenient and time-saving link to other sites or pages for information relative to that company. By taking advantage of the power of the Internet for access to many financial sites, PowerOptions acts as an options portal to provide most of the information needed to manage your naked put investments.

Some Cautions

This may sound too easy to be true. And usually when things look too easy or optimistic, there are traps waiting to catch you. That is the case here also. There are many things that can go wrong. A company may have a negative earnings surprise or a biotech company may not get FDA approval for its latest drug or maybe there is a patent suit issued against your favorite tech company. Any of these events can crash the price of your stock. In fact, if you screen or scan for companies based on high returns alone, you will find many of them are biotech firms that are very volatile and extremely risky. High returns generally mean high risk. A recent biotech firm was selling at $14 per share. The put with a strike of $10 had a return of 15 percent for one month out if the stock closed higher than the $10 strike price, which is almost 30 percent OTM. How could we go wrong? The stock would have to fall under $10 in the next 30 days to get us in any trouble. As time went by, the stock kept rising and hit $16 per share. This looked like a sure thing. But in one day, this stock gapped down from $16 to $6 per share because the FDA failed to approve its drug. This was a one-product drug discovery firm and the lack of FDA approval had a devastating impact on the company's prospects. Our sure thing turned into a disaster and a substantial loss. This stock now sells for under $1.

A positive example occurred with a stock that was selling at about $33 per share. We wrote 10 puts with a strike price of $30 that had a return of 10 percent for the following month. Annualized, this was more than a 100 percent per year return. Within several weeks, the stock gapped up from $34 to $95 because of a favorable announcement. At this point I was sorry that I did not just buy 1,000 shares of the stock. I would have had a gain of $61,000. Instead the put was worthless, and I made about $3,000 on the write. Eventually this stock came back down to $25. What a thrilling roller coaster ride this was both up and down. At least I made some money on it. Most people who write naked puts are interested in a secure source of income and do not want to speculate on the latest technology fad. Keep away from these situations unless you really know what you are doing and can accept the speculative risk.

Again remember there are no guarantees. Take a look at the illustration above on a down-trending stock. It shows arrows on the price graph that indicate earnings were going up while the stock was going down in price. There are no guarantees, even on earnings. What we are trying to do is increase the probability of success with our investments and to use tools to help in that effort. We use a hammer to build a house, but it can really hurt when you hit your finger with that same hammer.

Back Testing

One last thing to consider when using a screening program is the ability to back test your screening parameters. Some parameters are more important than others. If you can back test those parameters, it has the possibility of improving your investment results. Back testing can provide that extra level of confidence in the selection of parameters used for stock and option selection.

Back testing allows the user to test the validity of a screening process by applying the screening parameters to a historical data set representative of the market conditions in the past. Depending on what parameter values are chosen, different stocks would be considered for your Naked Put program. Back testing is another means to increase your probability of success.

As an example, in Figure 3.6, we have done a screen looking for naked puts with a return of 2 percent on stocks that are in an uptrend as measured by the stock price relative to the 50-day moving average and are 4 percent OTM. This screen was done based on the closing values, last year, on November 20, 2006, which was the day after the options expiration for November. We knew that the market was a little weak in December 2006 and wanted to know if going 4 percent OTM would give us enough downside protection while still allowing us to achieve the 2 percent per month target. So by using our screening parameters in the search named "Sample Screen," we found that four companies would have met our screening criteria.

But the question remained: How would these candidates have performed if they were all written as naked puts on November 20? Therefore, our next step would be to evaluate how these selections performed during the next month up to expiration. In this case, we

Figure 3.6 - Back Testing Results

Home	My Portfolio	Covered Call	Naked Put	Calendar Call	Bull Put Credit	Long Call	Bear Call Credit	Naked Call	Iron Condor	Other Strategies

Naked Puts Home | Option Chain | Search | Sample Searches | Search by Symbol | **Back Test** |

SmartHistoryXL Back Testing

Current Strategy	Naked Put	Change:	Naked Put
Search Date	« prev November 20, 2006 next »	Change:	Select Date
Saved Search Criteria	User Defined	Change:	None

Submit These Settings

* Expiration Day

For help getting started, view the SmartHistoryXL Instructions

Top 4 of 4 results for Naked Put search on November 20, 2006 ordered by % Naked Yield Annual   See More/Less Columns

More Info	Company Name	Stock Sym	Last Stock Price & Chg	Option Sym	Expire/Strike & Days To Exp	Opt Bid	% Naked Yield	% Naked Yield Annual	% Time Value	% Break Even	% In Money	% Prob. Above	Implied Volat.	Volat
	Focus Media Holding Ltd.	FMCN	59.86 (-1.87)	QOHXK	06 DEC 55.0 (26)	1.60	2.9	40.8	2.67	10.8	-8.1	70.1	0.61	0.39
	Arena Resources Inc	ARD	41.75 (+0.50)	ARDXH	06 DEC 40.0 (26)	1.15	2.9	40.4	2.75	6.9	-4.2	63.0	0.49	0.48
	Suntech Power Co. Ltd.	STP	26.60 (-0.40)	STPXE	06 DEC 25.0 (26)	0.60	2.4	33.7	2.26	8.3	-6	68.3	0.47	0.47
	MEMC Electronic Materials Inc.	WFR	37.04 (+0.73)	WFRXG	06 DEC 35.0 (26)	0.75	2.1	30.1	2.02	7.5	-5.5	69.7	0.43	0.45

Calculate Group Results

☐ Expired

Naked Put search filters   Save   Clear These Settings   Submit These Settings

Sort Results Table By		Greater Than	Less Than		Greater Than	Less Than
% Naked Yield Annual	% Naked Yield	2	to 30	% EPS Growth	20	to
Option Expiration Time Frame						
All Months	% Naked Yield Annual		to	Price/Earnings		to
Days To Expiration						
5 to 59	% Break Even		to	Price/Earnings/Growth		to
	% Break Even Annual		to	% Of 52 Week Range		to

Source: PowerOptions (www.poweropt.com)

were able to click on the "Calculate Group Results" button to obtain the results of the entire group of selections. The results are shown in Figure 3.7.

These selections turned out very good. All four of them were profitable and expired worthless. They all returned the maximum returns possible. Also note at the bottom of the results table the summary shows that the selections also performed better than the comparative averages over the same period of time. The QQQQ's were up only .1 percent and the S&P 500 was up only 1.9 percent, however, the

Figure 3.7 – Calculated Group Results From Back Testing Screen

Results for Naked Put search on November 20, 2006 using "User Defined" search settings   Custom End Date ▾

More Info		Co. Name	Stock Sym	Stock Price	Strike Mo.	Opt Sym	Opt Bid	% Naked Yield	End Date	Stock Price	Opt Ask	% In Money	Net Value	% Return
▶	☐	Focus Media Holding Ltd.	FMCN	59.86	06 DEC 55	QOHXK	1.60	2.9	12/15/2006	70.69	0.00	-22.2	0.00	2.9
▶	☐	Arena Resources Inc.	ARD	41.75	06 DEC 40	ARDXH	1.15	2.9	12/15/2006	44.70	0.00	-10.5	0.00	2.9
▶	☐	Suntech Power Co. Ltd.	STP	26.60	06 DEC 25	STPXE	0.60	2.4	12/15/2006	32.67	0.00	-23.5	0.00	2.4
▶	☐	MEMC Electronic Materials Inc.	WFR	37.04	06 DEC 35	WFRXG	0.75	2.1	12/15/2006	43.55	0.00	-19.6	0.00	2.1

Remove all checked results   [Remove]

Summary

 # Successful positions: 4 out of 4 (100%)
Avg. % Return: 2.6%
QQQQ % Return: 0.1% (11/20/2006 to 12/15/2006)
SPX % Return: 1.9% (11/20/2006 to 12/15/2006)

Source: PowerOptions (www.poweropt.com)

"Sample Screen" selections performed up 2.6 percent. In this case, our screening process produced a very successful group of stocks. Any of the selections would have worked out.

Another interesting observation about the results above can be seen from the % In Money column. All of these stocks performed up by double digits while the market in general as measured by the Q's or the S&P 500 hardly moved. The selection process would have been even more effective for an outright purchase of these stocks. But we are not speculators and should be happy with our 2.6 percent return in 26 days.

Chapter 4

FINDING THE "WRITE" NAKED PUT TRADE

NOW THAT WE HAVE INTRODUCED the general aspects of options, discussed the theoretical components of the naked put trade, and reviewed the methods of selecting neutral to bullish stocks as candidates for a naked put write, it is time to put it all together and apply that knowledge to finding, comparing, and analyzing a possible trade.

In this chapter we are not going to outline a specific trading methodology for writing (selling) naked puts. It is not our goal to give you a set of perfect criteria and then follow that up with "Always do this, never do that. If this occurs then follow with this. If this does not occur, always follow up with this. ..." It is our goal to help you learn the basics and fundamentals of the naked put trade so that you will have the knowledge of what to do in various situations. Our goal is to put you in control of your account, not to have that control in the hands of some advisor who really does not have your interests in mind.

Let's be honest, if we had the secret number or the lost key that opened the doors to 100 percent success rate in naked put trading, we would share it with you. Just like any form of investing, there is no secret number or magic key that will give you 100 percent success in any method of investing. The market moves in cycles and will change direction. Remember, the naked put investment strategy is best in neutral to bullish markets. In a raging bull market, you may have better returns simply investing in stocks or buying call options. In a raging bear market, you may be better off staying in cash, shorting stock, or buying put options.

The purpose of this text is to teach you how to fish so to speak, not to give you the fish cut, cleaned, and cooked only to have you find out the taste is not to your liking. Instead of being told by someone that you only like tuna prepared a certain way and do not need to taste any other fish, wouldn't you rather sample other kinds of fish prepared different ways so you can make up your own mind which style best matches your personal tastes?

There are many ways investors can trade this strategy from the most conservative style to a fairly aggressive style. We want to outline for you what criteria you can use, how they interact with one another, what are considered "reasonable" expectations for a naked put investor, and what you should expect to give up in terms of safety or protection when you seek a higher return trade.

Before we get directly into the criteria, let's recap the important points that were made in Chapter 2 and Chapter 3.

GENERAL REVIEW
Naked Put Theory:

- It is more conservative to write (sell) OTM or ATM naked puts.

- Selling an OTM put allows us to potentially buy stock at a discount.

- The naked put with the highest premium is not always the best trade.

- Percent to break even is the measure of protection for a naked put trade.

- Percent naked yield is the measure of return for a naked put trade.

- Selling naked puts month-by-month will yield a higher annualized return.

- Put options with a higher implied volatility offer an inflated premium, but greater potential risk.

- Delta measures the change in option premium compared to a one-point movement in the underlying security. Put options have a negative delta, meaning the premiums will decline in value when the stock price rises.

- Theta measures the rate the option premium will decay over time. Put options with a higher implied volatility and an inflated time value premium will have a higher theta value.

Stock Selection:

- Try to identify a stock you would not mind owning.

- Look for stocks currently in a 50-day uptrend.

- Look for companies with good management as measured by a growth in sales and earnings.

- Try to avoid companies with negative news reports, upcoming FDA rulings, or companies involved in a court proceeding.

Even with these points in mind, naked put investors typically approach a possible trade from one of two avenues. These two groups were previously discussed in Chapter 2: Investors in Group 1 have already researched a security and have a set price where they would want to purchase those shares, whereas investors in Group 2 are looking to find naked put opportunities that exist in the market based on their personal risk-reward tolerances.

An investor in Group 1 may simply use the broker's option chain tool to view the premium that is available for the put they wish to sell. However, most option chain tools offer limited criteria for analyzing options. The information available may only consist of the strike price, expiration month, option symbol, the puts bid and ask price, current volume, and open interest. If the investor is lucky, the broker might also display the delta and theta for the put option.

For a serious naked put investor, this data is not nearly sufficient to thoroughly research and compare between the different puts that are available on the stock. Yes, we will admit that if the investor's target price is $40.00 for a stock that is trading at $47.00, he or she will simply look to sell the 40 strike put for the next expiration month, regardless of the premium that is available. The investor will be able to obtain the price and liquidity data from a simple chain, but will not be able to compare the probability, implied volatility, percent to break even, percent naked yield, annualized percent naked yield, or the advanced Greeks for the put option he or she is preparing to sell.

Throughout Chapter 2, we used several screen shots from the PowerOptions option chain to help define the important theoretical

Figure 4.1 – Option Chain for FRPT With Essential Naked Put Criteria

Strike	Put Sym	Opt Bid	Opt Ask	Black Sch.	B-S Ratio 50 Dev	Curr Opt Vol	Prev Opt Vol	Open Int	Implied Volat	% Imp Volat Range	% Break Even	% Naked Yield	% Naked Ann	% Prob Above	% Time Value	% In Money	Delta	Theta
Force Protection Inc. (FRPT) $23.56						AUGUST		Expiring 8/18/2007	38 days left									Hold ☑
20.00	QFZTD	0.95	1.00	0.63	1.78	10	17	444	0.87	52%	19.9%	4.8%	45.6%	73.0%	4.0%	-15.1%	-0.22	-0.0237
22.50	QFZTX	2.25	2.40	1.73	1.30	77	23	480	0.86	51%	11.9%	10.0%	96.1%	51.2%	9.9%	-0.8%	-0.43	-0.0304
25.00	QFZTE	3.70	4.00	3.26	1.14	10	0	475	0.86	59%	7.3%	5.1%	48.9%	36.1%	6.1%	10.2%	-0.58	-0.0297
30.00	QFZTF	7.60	7.90	7.40	1.03	0	0	42	0.85	47%	1.9%	0.8%	7.5%	15.3%	1.3%	32.2%	-0.81	-0.0189
Force Protection Inc. (FRPT) $23.56						SEPTEMBER		Expiring 9/22/2007	73 days left									Hold ☑
15.00	QFZUC	0.50	0.65	0.17	2.97	0	0	152	0.91	69%	36.9%	3.3%	16.7%	86.2%	2.2%	-33.9%	-0.10	-0.0097
17.50	QFZUW	1.05	1.15	0.54	1.94	0	10	178	0.87	49%	28.8%	6.0%	30.0%	75.3%	4.6%	-22.9%	-0.18	-0.0150
20.00	QFZUD	1.60	1.80	1.27	1.46	11	102	881	0.84	70%	21.8%	8.0%	40.0%	63.0%	8.2%	-11.9%	-0.29	-0.0191
25.00	QFZUE	4.50	4.60	3.89	1.16	17	260	1822	0.81	62%	12.0%	9.1%	45.5%	39.9%	9.7%	10.2%	-0.52	-0.0213
30.00	QFZUF	8.10	8.40	7.73	1.05	0	0	75	0.81	62%	5.4%	2.1%	10.6%	23.0%	3.5%	32.2%	-0.70	-0.0173

Source: PowerOptions (www.poweropt.com)

components of a put option. With each new screen shot, we were able to display only those data columns that pertained to the theoretical component that was being introduced. The PowerOptions option chain is unique because it allows the investor to customize the data columns displayed so the results field is personalized for the investor's individual needs.

The field in Figure 4.1 shows the options criteria that were discussed in Chapter 2. These criteria are the fundamental data that a naked put investor should use to identify and evaluate the risk-reward values for a potential position. The essential criteria for analyzing the price movements of the put options are also displayed.

IDENTIFICATION PARAMETERS

The first data column is the strike price of the put (the price we are obligated to pay for the stock). The second data column is the exchange symbol for the put option. The option symbol identifies the underlying stock (first letters), the expiration month (second to last letter), and the strike price of the put option (last letter). Figure 4.1 shows the symbol for the August expiration 20 strike put is **QFZTD.**

Here is a breakdown of the option symbol notation:

QFZ – These first three symbols are the option root symbol for the underlying stock, FRTP.

T – The second to last letter signifies the option is a put option for the August expiration month. Options with letters M through Z in the second to last letter identify them as put options and the expiration month.

D – This letter signifies that this is the 20 strike option for the FRPT series.

When placing an order you want to verify that you have entered in the correct symbol. Next time you are at your computer, take a look at your keyboard. Notice the D key is right next to the E, F, and X key. If the wrong key were accidentally hit when entering the trade, the whole dynamic of the position would be altered. Tips and techniques on placing the trade will be discussed in the next chapter.

REWARD PARAMETERS

Premium

The third and fourth data columns shown in Figure 4.1 are the bid and ask price for the option. When selling (writing) a naked put, the investor will typically receive the bid price while an option buyer will pay the ask price for a market order. If an option has a wide bid-ask spread, an investor may be able to place a limit order to try and get a slightly higher bid price when selling the option or slightly lower ask price when buying the option.

The bid price is the monetary value an investor receives for selling the put contract. Regardless of the strike price that has been selected as the target price for buying shares of the underlying stock, the investor still needs to make sure that the bid price for the put option will cover the transaction costs.

For example, if QFZTD had a bid price of $0.05 and only one contract was sold, the transaction costs, including commissions and other fees, would have to be less than $5.00 in order to have the potential of earning a profit.

To determine how many contracts can be sold, simply divide the capital value available for the trade by the potential strike price times 100.

# of Contracts to Sell = Available Capital / (Strike Price * 100)

If $5,000 was available to place a trade and an investor was considering selling the QFZTD August 20 strike put, then:

# of Contracts to Sell = ($5,000) / (20 * 100)

# of Contracts to Sell = ($5,000) / (2,000)

# of Contracts to Sell = 2.5, or 2 contracts as one cannot sell half a contract

This method of determining how many contracts could be sold is based on the recommendation that the investor is totally cash-secured for the trade.

Percent Naked Yield

The next parameters that determine the reward for the naked put trade are the percent naked yield and the annualized percent naked yield, the 13th and 14th data columns, respectively. Although the bid price shows the monetary value that would be earned for selling the put contract, the percent naked yield is a better parameter to use when evaluating a trade as it shows the premium received as a percentage of the required capital.

Figure 4.1 shows QFZTD 20 strike put with a bid price of $0.95. This trade would have a potential 4.8 percent naked yield.

Percent Naked Yield = Premium / Strike Price

Percent Naked Yield = $0.95 / 20

Percent Naked Yield = 4.8%, rounded up from 4.75%

When comparing between different trades, the percent naked yield would be a better gauge of return instead of the option premium.

Let's look at a quick example.

Stock XYZ is trading at $23.00
One month out 20 strike put is trading for $0.95
Percent Naked Yield = 4.8% ($0.95 / 20)

Stock ABC is trading at $58.00
One month out 55 strike put is trading for $0.95
Percent Naked Yield = 1.7% ($0.95 / 55)

If the investor were neutral to bullish on both stocks, the XYZ trade would be the better selection. Even though the same monetary amount could be collected for selling either put, the percent naked yield on the XYZ is much higher due to the lower capital requirement.

Percent Naked Yield Annualized

The percent naked yield annualized is necessary to view when comparing the same strike price on an underlying security in different expiration months. From Figure 4.1 we see that the August 20 strike put has 38 days left to expiration and has a percent naked yield annualized of 45.6 percent. This means that if the 20 strike put was sold for $0.95 every 38 days, the return after one year would be 45.6 percent.

In comparison, the September 20 strike put has 73 days left to expiration and could be sold for $1.60. The percent naked yield is 8.0 percent, almost twice the return of the August 20 strike put. However, the percent naked yield annualized is only 40.0 percent. If the two-month out 20 strike put was sold every 73 days for a premium of $1.60, the annualized return would be lower than the one-month out put of the same strike.

> **Trading Tip:** When selling options in an income-generating strategy such as naked puts, covered calls, credit spreads, or calendar spreads, it is recommended to sell the option with the shortest time period to expiration, usually within 45 days to expiration. Ninety-nine percent of the time, the shorter-term options will have a higher annualized return over the options that are further out in time.

There are, however, rare occurrences when it is of a greater advantage to sell a put option that is further out in time.

In Figure 4.2 we have reduced the data columns for an easier view of the important fields. Figure 4.2 shows that the December 2.5 strike put is selling for $0.60. This could potentially yield a 24.0 percent return (over 137 days) and a percent naked yield annualized return of 63.9 percent.

In comparison, the 2008 January 2.5 strike put is selling for $2.50 with a potential return of 48.0 percent (over 165 days). This would give a percent naked yield annualized return of 106.2 percent, nearly doubling the December annualized yield.

Figure 4.2 - December 2007 and January 2008 Put Chain for GTOP

Strike	Put Sym	Opt Bid	Opt Ask	Implied Volat.	% Naked Yield	% Naked Ann.	% Prob. Above	% In Money
Genitope Corp. (GTOP) $ 3.45			DECEMBER Expiring 12/22/2007 137 days left					Hold ☑
2.50	GWYXZ	0.60	0.80	1.55	24.0%	63.9%	92.4%	-27.5%
5.00	GWYXA	2.25	2.45	1.54	10.7%	28.3%	4.9%	44.9%
7.50	GWYXU	4.30	4.70	1.60	2.2%	5.7%	0.1%	117.4%
10.00	GWYXB	6.70	7.00	1.72	0.9%	2.4%	0.1%	189.9%
12.50	GWYXV	9.00	9.40	1.76	-0.2%	-0.6%	0.1%	282.3%
Genitope Corp. (GTOP) $ 3.45			JANUARY Expiring 1/19/2008 165 days left					Hold ☑
2.50	GWYMZ	1.20	1.40	2.50	46.0%	106.2%	90.4%	-27.5%
5.00	GWYMA	3.40	3.60	2.82	26.2%	62.1%	6.6%	44.9%
7.50	GWYMU	5.30	5.60	2.53	10.8%	23.8%	0.1%	117.4%
10.00	GWYMB	7.40	7.70	2.38	5.1%	11.3%	0.1%	189.9%
12.50	GWYMV	9.70	10.00	2.39	3.0%	6.6%	0.1%	282.3%
15.00	GWYMC	11.90	12.30	2.31	1.3%	2.9%	0.1%	334.8%
17.50	GWYMW	14.20	14.70	2.31	0.5%	1.0%	0.1%	407.2%

Source: PowerOptions (www.poweropt.com)

This anomaly exists because the FDA is expected to rule on a Phase III trial of a GTOP drug in January. This expected event has driven the implied volatility of the January options above 2.50 (250 percent). The December options also have a high implied volatility, around 1.55 (155 percent). Although this example shows the rare scenario where the far out option has a higher annualized percentage return, the options listed are extremely risky due to the future event. The increased premium generally does not compensate for the increased risk. These types of risky trades should be avoided as large losses could be realized in spite of the inflated premiums.

Percent Time Value

Time value and percent time value are other criteria that can be used to measure the reward of a naked put trade. As discussed in Chapter 2, the time value of an OTM put option is equal to the listed bid price as there is no intrinsic value. The percent time value is the percentage of the time value compared to the value of the underlying security.

The percent time value can be a useful criterion to use when comparing the return between potential trades. However, the percent naked yield is a more effective criterion to use when selecting a naked put trade because it compares the premium received to the strike price of the sold put. Thus, the percent naked yield is a more accurate percentage when evaluating the reward of the trade against the actual obligation of selling the put option.

What to Look for

Although you want to make sure that the bid price (premium) you receive for the trade will at least cover your transaction costs, the reward values for the bid price, percent naked yield, and percent naked yield annualized should be determined by the individual investor. The goal of the Group 1 investor is to buy shares of stock at a discount. Once the target price for the stock has been selected, the investor may simply choose to sell (write) the put option with the closest strike price to the target price that was determined. In this scenario, the percent naked yields and percent time value are important values to use to compare between the different expiration months, but the main goal is to sell the put option that best correlates to the target price for the underlying security.

In contrast, Group 2 investors will be more focused on the percent naked yield and the percent naked yield annualized returns. The Group 2 investors are looking for bullish to neutral stock candidates but they are not looking to buy shares of that stock at a discount. These investors want to take advantage of the current trend without investing in the underlying security. If a Group 2 investor is hoping to achieve a 24 to 36 percent annualized return, they will only look for the naked put trades that offer a 2 to 3 percent naked yield on a monthly basis.

Whether an investor falls into the Group 1 or Group 2 investment style, he or she can still choose to be conservative, moderate, or aggressive when selling naked puts. Over the years, we have been asked several times: "What should I look for when selling a naked put? What is the average return and average protection I should expect to get?"

These are not easy questions to answer, but we can estimate the expected returns, protection, and probabilities of earning that return using the Black-Scholes calculator. Remember, the Black-Scholes pricing model calculates the theoretical worth of an option using five criteria: stock price, strike price of the option, days remaining to expiration, interest rates, and the stock's historical volatility.

One of the tools on PowerOptions is the Optionable Stock Statistics page. This shows the average values of specific criteria across all optionable stocks and all options for those stocks. Using the Optionable Stock Statistics page, we see that the average stock price for all optionable stocks is currently $34.50. The average volatility for all optionable stocks is 0.35 (35 percent). We have stated that a naked put investor will look to sell put options that are 30 to 45 days out in time to maximize the annualized return. The current interest rates are about 4.5 percent. These were the market averages during the early spring of 2007.

If we input these average criteria into the Black-Scholes calculator, we can calculate the theoretical option premiums for different strike prices on that stock, and then calculate the expected percent naked yield and other risk-reward values for those positions.

DIFFERENT INVESTMENT STYLES

Stock XYZ is trading at $34.50 (the average stock price for all optionable stocks).

Volatility on stock XYZ is 0.35 (35 percent).

Current interest rates are 4.5 percent.

Next month out options series has 40 days remaining to expiration.

Conservative Naked Put Trade:
Sell the 30 Strike Put (2 Strikes OTM).
Theoretical Black-Scholes Value: $0.20.
Percent Naked Yield: 0.6% ($0.20 / 30).

Moderate Naked Put Trade:
Sell the 32.5 Strike Put (1 Strike OTM).
Theoretical Black-Scholes Value: $0.70
Percent Naked Yield: 2.1% ($0.70 / 32.5)

Aggressive Naked Put Trade:
Sell the 35 Strike Put (Slightly ITM).
Theoretical Black Scholes Value: $1.75
Percent Naked Yield: 3.5% ($1.25 / 35)

Remember, since the 35 strike put is $0.50 in-the-money, we are giving up $0.50 of intrinsic value at the time of the trade. The profit for an ITM naked put trade is the time value, not the total premium received.

Is this to say that all naked put trades with a percent naked yield less than 2 percent are conservative and that all naked put trades with a percent naked yield greater than 3.5 percent are aggressive? Absolutely not. There are several other factors involved with a naked put trade that help define the risk-reward ratio for the trade. The values above are merely the return values (reward) an investor could expect to receive based on the average values across the entire universe of options. An investor cannot determine the risk-reward ratio for a potential trade by just examining the reward values.

RISK ASSESSMENT PARAMETERS

When entering a naked put trade, an investor needs to have an entry and exit strategy already in place. The risk assessment parameters give naked put investors the values needed to track and monitor their exit points.

Percent to Break Even

The *percent to break even* may be the most important criteria to use when researching a naked put trade. This parameter shows how far the underlying security can drop in value before the position reaches the break-even point.

In Chapter 2 we discussed the percent to break even equation and outlined a few examples:

**% to Break Even = Stock Price – Break Even/Stock Price
(Where the Break Even = Put Option Strike Price – Premium
Received)**

The percent to break even is the true level of protection for the naked put trade. The higher the percent to break even, the further the stock can decline in value before the trade is technically losing value. If the percent to break even is relatively low, the investor has little or no protection on the trade. The underlying security would only need to fall a small amount before the investor loses money on the trade.

Applying this concept to the three styles of naked put, we can generally state that a percent to break even higher than 8 percent would be considered conservative, a percent to break even between 4 percent and 8 percent would be fairly moderate, and a percent to break even of less than 3 percent would be fairly aggressive. When one is considering selling a naked put, one should make sure the protection level matches one's risk-reward threshold.

Percent Out-of-the-Money (OTM)

The *percent out-of-the-money* value is similar to the percent to break even. The percent OTM value shows how far the put strike is below the current stock price. This reflects how far the stock can drop in value before the stock reaches the put strike price, but it does not take into account the premium received for selling the put contract, which further hedges the position.

Naked put investors in Group 2 are more likely to use the percent OTM value over the percent to break even because they do not want the stock to be *put* to them. The Group 2 investors will normally use the put strike price as the stop/loss point for the trade to avoid having the option go in-the-money and risk having to purchase shares of the underlying security. Therefore, they are more concerned with the percent OTM than the percent to break even for the trade.

Percent Probability Above

This value shows the investor the theoretical probability that the stock will be trading at or above the sold put strike price at expiration. Put more simply, this shows the investor the theoretical probability of success on the trade. Of course, different investors have different definitions of what is a successful trade.

An investor from Group 2 might consider the trade successful if the stock remains above the put strike price at expiration and the option expires worthless. An investor in Group 1 would also consider this scenario a success, but having the stock *put* to them at their designated target price might also be considered a success. In general, in any options strategy where a premium or net credit is received, the goal of the trade is to achieve the maximum possible profit. In a naked put trade, the maximum profit is achieved when the option expires worthless. This is why we refer to the percent probability above as the theoretical probability of success on the trade.

Even though the percent probability above is based on the historical trading range of the underlying security, there is an obvious relationship between the probability and the percent OTM. Deeper OTM puts will have a higher probability of success, as it is unlikely that the underlying security will have a drastic drop in the next 30 days. Put options that are at-the-money (ATM) will roughly have a 50 percent chance of being successful. This reflects the general idea of any form of investing: The higher the reward, the greater the risk. The greater the safety, the lower the potential return.

EXPECT THE BEST RISK-REWARD RATIO ... WITHIN REASON

This brings us to the relationship between the three risk assessment criteria and the reward criteria. As investors, we want to receive the most return with the least amount of risk in every trade. We want the perfect scenario for our investments, but we have to be reasonable in our expectations. A knowledgeable investor will not expect to receive a 10 percent monthly return on a naked put trade and have a 95 percent probability of success. If the trades were that easy, every investor would apply to trade naked puts.

What are the reasonable risk-reward ratios that a naked put investor should expect?

To answer that question, let's refer back to the example shown in the reward section, which used the average values of all optionable stocks. We used the Black-Scholes pricing model to calculate the theoretical option price to determine the percent naked yield for each potential trade. We can also use that information to determine the percent to break even and percent OTM range:

Stock XYZ is trading at $34.50.

Volatility on stock XYZ is 0.35 (35%).

Current interest rates are 4.5%.

Next month out options series has 40 days remaining to expiration.

Conservative Naked Put Trade:
Sell the 30 strike Put (2 Strikes OTM).
Theoretical Black-Scholes Value: $0.20.
Percent Naked Yield: 0.6% ($0.20 / 30).
Percent to Break Even: 13.6% ($34.50 - $29.80 / $34.50).
Percent OTM: 13.0% ($34.50 - $30.00 / $30.00).
Percent Probability Above: 88.6% (Calculated using the Black-Scholes Calculator).

Moderate Naked Put Trade:

Sell the 32.5 Strike Put (1 Strike OTM).

Theoretical Black-Scholes Value: $0.70.

Percent Naked Yield: 2.1% ($0.70 / 32.5).

Percent to Break Even: 7.8% ($34.50 - $31.80 / $34.50).

Percent OTM: 5.8% ($34.50 - $32.50 / $34.50).

Percent Probability Above: 69.6% (Calculated using the Black-Scholes Calculator).

Aggressive Naked Put Trade:

Sell the 35 Strike Put (Slightly ITM).

Theoretical Black Scholes Value: $1.75.

Percent Naked Yield: 3.5% ($1.25 / 35).

Percent to Break Even: 3.6% ($34.50 – $33.25 / $34.50).

Percent OTM: -1.4% ($34.50 - $35.00 / $34.50).

Percent Probability Above: 45% (Calculated using the Black-Scholes Calculator).

Based on average-priced stock and average market volatility, we see that the conservative naked put trade potentially has a 0.6 percent return with a 13.6 percent protection. Although the return may be considered low by some investors, there is roughly a 90 percent chance that the 0.6 percent return will be achieved.

In contrast, the aggressive naked put trade offers a much higher 3.5 percent return but only a 3.6 percent protection. And although the return is significantly higher, there is only a 45 percent chance that the 3.5 percent return will be achieved.

This example showcases the definitions from Chapter 2. A conservative naked put trade offers a decent return, high protection, and a high probability of earning that return. The aggressive naked put trade offers a high potential return, low protection, and a small probability of earning that return.

Table 4.1 shows the risk-reward assessment values for the conservative, moderate, and aggressive naked put trade based on the theoretical premiums calculated on stock XYZ trading at $34.50 with a volatility of 0.38.

Table 4.1 – Risk-Reward Assessment

Trade Type	Strike	Premium	% Yield	% to BE	%OTM	% Prob.
Conservative	30	$0.20	0.6%	13.6%	13.0%	88.6%
Moderate	32.5	$0.70	2.1%	7.8%	5.8%	69.6%
Aggressive	35	$1.75	3.5%	3.6%	-1.4%	45.0%

If an investor wants to receive the higher return, he or she will have to give up some protection and accept the lower probability of earning that return, just like with any other type of investment. An investor would be hard-pressed to find a naked put trade that offered a return of 4 percent or more that also offered a 10 percent protection and a 90 percent probability of earning that 4 percent return within a 30 to 45 day time period. That is simply how the market works.

"But wait," you might be thinking. "The QFZTD example from Figure 4.1 has a percent naked yield of 4.8 percent, a percent to break even (protection) of 19.9 percent, and a 73 percent probability above. That trade offers a high return, great protection, and a strong probability of being successful."

You bring up a very valid point. In fact, to demonstrate further examples we ran the aforementioned criteria in the SmartSearchXL tool introduced in Chapter 3. Ignoring the stock criteria outlined in Chapter 3, we searched for naked puts that had a minimum 4 percent naked yield, minimum 10 percent protection (percent to break even), and at least a 90 percent theoretical percent probability above between 30 to 45 days remaining to expiration. To counter our own statements, the SmartSearchXL tool provided six naked put trades that matched these outstanding criteria.

								% Naked						
More Info	Company Name	Stock Sym	Last Stock Price & Chg	Option Sym	Expire/Strike & Days To Exp	Opt Bid	% Naked Yield	Yield Annual	% Time Value	% Break Even	% In Money	% Prob. Above	Implied Volat.	Volat
	Indy Mac Bancorp	IMB	19.44 (-0.69)	IMBUA	07 SEP 5.0 (39)	0.25	5.0	46.8	1.29	75.6	-74.3	99.8	3.04	0.54
	Indy Mac Bancorp	IMB	19.44 (-0.69)	IMBUU	07 SEP 7.5 (39)	0.60	8.0	74.9	3.09	64.5	-61.4	97.8	2.79	0.54
	Indy Mac Bancorp	IMB	19.44 (-0.69)	IMBUB	07 SEP 10.0 (39)	1.05	10.5	98.3	5.4	54.0	-48.6	92.1	2.39	0.54
	Beazer Homes USA Inc	BZH	11.33 (-1.01)	BZHUA	07 SEP 5.0 (39)	0.50	10.0	93.6	4.41	60.3	-55.9	91.0	2.63	1.13
	Standard Pacific Corp.	SPF	10.15 (-0.58)	SPFUA	07 SEP 5.0 (39)	0.40	8.0	74.9	3.94	54.7	-50.7	91.0	2.22	0.73
	Sonus Pharmaceuticals Inc.	SNUS	4.20 (-0.26)	NUYUZ	07 SEP 2.5 (39)	0.15	6.0	56.2	3.57	44.0	-40.5	90.7	1.92	0.35

Figure 4.3 – Results for High Return, High Probability, and High Protection

Source: PowerOptions (www.poweropt.com)

The six positions in Figure 4.3 all match the required criteria. Naturally, this means these are the best positions to trade, right? Wrong. Everything about the trades in Figure 4.3 seems to be too good to be true: Fantastic returns, amazing protection, and extremely high probabilities of success.

This brings us to another rule of investing, and of life. "If a position appears too good to be true, it probably is not as good as it appears."

Implied Volatility—True Measure of Risk

The volatility of an underlying stock and the corresponding implied volatility of the option was detailed in Chapter 2. Companies with a proven track record and a multitude of successful products tend not to fluctuate in price as often as smaller companies with a smaller range of products or a less than stable revenue stream. Those companies with an unproven track record and an unstable revenue stream are riskier investments. This risk is measured by the historical volatility of the stock, and is reflected in the implied volatility of the options for that stock. An option's implied volatility also reflects any near-term events that may cause a sudden shift in the underlying stock price: earnings announcements, FDA rulings, or patent infringement lawsuits against the company.

Figure 4.3 shows the available trades that matched the outstanding criteria of a potential best-case scenario. The second to last and last columns of Figure 4.3 show the implied volatility of the options and the historical volatility of the stock. The lowest implied volatility of those naked put trades that matched the outstanding criteria is 1.92, or 192 percent. This is more than five times the average implied volatility of all options across the entire universe of options!

These potential naked put trades that match the criteria of high potential percent naked yield, high percent to break even, and a high percent probability above all have an extremely high risk factor. Whether this risk is due to a pending earnings announcement, an FDA approval, or a pending court decision is irrelevant. What is relevant is that the market's speculation on these pending near-term events could cause the underlying security to rise or fall significantly due to the outcome of that event. These potential trades that match the "best case" scenario for the naked put strategy carry too high of a potential risk and should be avoided.

There are different reasons why the historical volatilities of these stocks and the implied volatilities of their respective options are so high. Three of the underlying stocks that matched the criteria, Indy Mac Bancorp (IMB), Beazer Homes (BZH), and Standard Pacific Corp. (SPF), are in the mortgage lending and home building industries. Due to recent problems with sub-prime mortgages and the housing sector in general, the risk in these types of investments is very high.

The fourth stock on the list, Sonus Pharmaceuticals Inc. (SNUS), is going to release the results of its Phase III drug trial near the end of September. This near-term event greatly increases the risk of trading the September options. If the results of the trial come out prior to September expiration, the stock could move significantly in either direction. If the results of the trial are not favorable, the stock could quickly decline in value and the investor may end up holding shares of stock that are relatively worthless. Although the potential return is very high, the inherent risk is overwhelming. These types of high-risk trades are better suited for other strategies such as long straddles, where the speculative trader bets that the stock will swing in price one direction or the other. Naked put investors will avoid these types of risky investments and find trades that are much less speculative.

One way to avoid riskier stocks with inflated premiums because of concerns about a company's sector or industry or an upcoming event is to restrict the range of volatility for the stock or the implied volatility for the option. Previously we used the average stock price of all optionable stocks and their average volatility to calculate the risk and reward expectations for a conservative, moderate, and aggressive naked put trade.

To avoid unnecessary risk, one rule of thumb is to only screen for stocks that have a historical volatility less than twice the average of all optionable stocks. If the average historical volatility is 0.38 (38 percent), you might consider filtering your stock candidates to those with an historical volatility less than 0.76 (76 percent). To be more conservative, you might want to restrict your candidates to only those stocks with a historical volatility below 0.60 (60 percent). More aggressive investors might increase the upper limit based on their personal risk-reward tolerance.

There are some occasions in which the implied volatility of the option is much higher than the historical volatility of the underlying security. The historical volatility reflects how frequently the stock has fluctuated in price. It is an indicator of the changes in the stock price over a set period of time. The implied volatility of the option is an indication of the market's expectation of the future volatility of the underlying security. Even though the stock might have a relatively stable trading range, the outcome of a near-term event will increase the risk on the options that expire prior to that event.

The results in Figure 4.3 display this relationship. Indy Mac Bancorp (IMB) has an historical volatility of 0.54 (54 percent). This value would meet the conservative criteria mentioned for restricting the volatility to be less than 0.60 (60 percent). However, the three September put options for IMB have an average implied volatility of 2.69 (269 percent). The same inconsistency can be seen on the potential naked put trade on Sonus Pharmaceuticals Inc. (SNUS). The historical volatility for SNUS is only 0.35 (35 percent), slightly below the average for all optionable stocks. However, the implied volatility for the September option that matched the criteria is 1.92 (almost 200 percent)! Even though SNUS has not fluctuated in price that frequently over the historical time frame, the pending results from the Phase III drug trial greatly enhance the risk of trading options in the September expiration month.

This is why it is always a good idea when selecting potential naked put trades to avoid options with a high implied volatility in addition to avoiding stocks with a high historical volatility. The same general rule of thumb regarding the historical volatility can be applied to restricting the implied volatility. A naked put investor who wants to avoid any unexpected fluctuations in the stock price due to a pending event might not sell a put option with an implied volatility more than twice the average of all options in the market. If the average implied volatility for all options is 0.35 (35 percent), an investor might only consider selling put options that have an implied volatility less than 0.70 (70 percent). Again, a more conservative investor might lower this restriction to find only those options with an implied volatility less than 0.60 (60 percent); where a more aggressive trader might increase this value if he or she wished to find investments that carried a higher risk with a potentially higher return.

> **Trading Tip:** The general rules of thumb for filtering the historical volatility for the stock and the implied volatility for the option are predicated on the investor knowing the average value for these criteria across the entire market. An investor might find these values through exhaustive searching of various data sources. PowerOptions subscribers can access the average volatility values (and the average values for more than 40 other criteria) using the Optionable Stock Statistics Page included in the PowerOptions suite of tools.

Avoiding stocks with a high historical volatility and options with an increased implied volatility will help you avoid any unexpected surprises during the expiration period. However, simply restricting the criteria is not a replacement for research and due diligence. Once you have found a potential trade, you will still need to research the underlying security to determine if there are any pending circumstances or upcoming events that might affect your trade. Limiting the volatility values will reduce the number of potential trades that you will need to research when determining which position matches your investment strategy. There may be other risks involved that are not reflected in the volatility values but can be avoided with proper research and investigation into the underlying security.

Overvalued/Undervalued Options

Another important aspect an investor needs to assess before selling a naked put is if the option is overvalued or undervalued. The previous sections have discussed the criteria one should use when analyzing the risk-reward ratios for a naked put trade. In this strategy, we are selling a contract to the market. Even if the premium offered matches our personal risk-reward tolerance, we still want to receive a good value for the contract we are selling. If you were planning on selling your house or your car, would you not try to receive better than market value for your property? Of course you would, and you should expect nothing less when you are selling a put contract.

In Chapter 2 we walked you through the concepts of the Black-Scholes value of an option and the values used in the Black-Scholes pricing model. The Black-Scholes value is the theoretical value for a specific option. As mentioned before, option contracts typically do not trade on the market at the theoretical price. The simplest way to determine if an option is overvalued or undervalued is to use the *Black-Scholes Ratio*. This ratio compares the actual trading price of the option to its theoretical worth:

Black-Scholes Ratio = Trading Price of the Option/Theoretical Worth

If the option we are researching has a Black-Scholes Ratio equal to 1, the trading price of the option is equal to its theoretical worth. An option with a Black-Scholes Ratio of 1.25 means that the trading price of the option is 25 percent higher than its theoretical worth (25 percent overvalued). An option with a Black-Scholes Ratio of 0.75

means that the trading price of the option is 25 percent less than its theoretical value (25 percent undervalued).

As option sellers, we want to look for overvalued options. We want to get more bang for our buck, so to speak. We want to collect more premium than the option is theoretically worth. If you are a Group 1 investor and have already picked the stock and the target price to purchase shares of stock, this criterion does not necessarily apply. You are going to sell the strike that is closest to the target price you selected to buy shares of stock. Investors in Group 2 will want to look for put options that have a Black-Scholes Ratio greater than 1 to find only those options that are overvalued.

The Trading Tip in the volatility discussion of Chapter 2 pointed out that there are many different time frames that can be used to measure volatility. As volatility is one of the main components of the Black-Scholes equation, there are also different Black-Scholes values for an option depending on the measure of volatility that is used. Naked put investors typically focus on the option that has less than 45 days to expiration to maximize the annualized return. Therefore, it is best to use the 50-day volatility when calculating the Black-Scholes value to compare against the trading price of the option, or to use the Stocks Implied Volatility Index (SIV) value, which is the average implied volatility of the ITM and OTM calls and puts of the near term expiration months. The 50-day volatility and the SIV are better indicators to evaluate the near term options compared to the longer-term volatility measures over 100, 200, or 250 days.

Another method investors use to evaluate if the option is overvalued or undervalued is to compare the option's implied volatility to the underlying stock's historical volatility. The historical volatility reflects the past price fluctuations of the stock itself. The option's implied volatility measures the market's future expectation of the stock's volatility pending the outcome of any near-term events. The implied volatility ratio is the ratio of the implied volatility (the future expectation of volatility) divided by the historical volatility (the past volatility of the stock). If the implied volatility ratio is greater than 1, many investors surmise that the option is overvalued because the future expectation of the volatility is greater than the past volatility. In contrast, if the implied volatility ratio is less than 1, the future expectation of the volatility is less than the past volatility; therefore, the option is under-valued. Naked put investors want to find overvalued options, so we would look for an implied volatility ratio greater than 1.

Either the Black-Scholes Ratio or the implied volatility ratio can be used to help determine if the option is overvalued or undervalued. An investor can even use both criteria when screening for overvalued options, though it is not necessary.

Evaluating the Risk-Reward Ratios

When writing naked puts, just like any other form of investment, one has to be aware of the realistic expectations when searching for or placing a trade. In this chapter we have outlined for you the gen-eralized expectations for the risk-reward tolerance when placing a conservative, moderate, or aggressive naked put trade based on the average stock price of all optionable stocks and the average volatility on those stocks. All stocks do not have the same price nor do they have the same volatility. In addition, many optionable stocks will have upcoming events that will inflate the price of the near term puts, which is reflected in the implied volatility. This is why we sometimes define implied volatility as the double-edged sword.

Options that have a higher implied volatility also have a higher potential percent naked yield and a greater percent to break even because of the inflated premium. This works to the advantage of a naked put writer, as these trades will offer a better risk-reward ratio. However, if the implied volatility is too high, the potential risk for the trade might not outweigh the benefit of the higher premium. If you stumble across a naked put position that is offering a return and protection that seem too good to be true, then it probably is. The option is highly overvalued for a reason, most likely because of the risk involved with trading that option. When you find a trade of this kind, the first thing you should do is check the implied volatility for the option. Most likely, the implied volatility will be well above twice the average of all options across the market. The increased implied volatility will alert you that there is an upcoming event that may cause a drastic shift in the underlying stock price. You can then research the company news to determine the nature of the upcoming event, and from that research decide if the risk for the trade is within your personal threshold.

Liquidity and the Greeks

In Chapter 2, we outlined some general rules of thumb regarding the option volume and the open interest. The suggested values will help filter out thinly traded options that may have a deflated premium or may cause problems when the investor is attempting to close or adjust the trade. Many investors already have their own minimum requirements for volume and open interest set when they plan to enter a trade. Just as some stock investors will not trade a stock if the average volume is less than 500,000 shares per day, many experienced options investors will not sell or buy an option if the daily volume is less than 50, 100, or even 1,000 contracts. The same holds true for the open interest.

Through the years, we have also talked with dozens of "bargain hunt-ers." These investors will screen specifically for options with little or no volume and low open interest. Their concept is that they can place a limit order for the option and get a better price from the market maker, as there is no interest on the particular option. This type of investing is more aggressive and has a few drawbacks. First, if the option has not traded in some time, the listed price might not have been updated recently. This means that the limit order might never get filled, or worse, if you placed the trade as a market order you might receive a premium that is vastly lower from the listed price. Second, if there is little or no liquidity you may have a harder time trying to exit the position if the stock starts to move against you.

As you become a more active options investor, you will develop your own limitations and requirements for option volume and open interest based on the success rate of your trades. If you are just starting out and you are looking to place your first trade, we suggest following the recommendations in Chapter 2: Screen for positions that have a volume that is at least 5 times greater than the number of contracts you are hoping to sell, and an open interest at least 10 times greater than the number of contracts you are hoping to sell.

Knowledge of the Greeks is essential to any options trader regardless of the options strategy you are trading. The Greeks give investors advanced insight into how the option premiums may adjust with changes in the stock price, time decay, volatility, or fluctuations in the interest rate. Even though the delta and theta values are important to know when entering or monitoring a naked put trade, there are no real guidelines one should follow when screening for positions.

If you are selling a naked put that is three or more strikes OTM, the delta for the option will be relatively low. The deeper OTM put options will have a delta closer to 0 (zero). ATM put options, those closest to the stock price, will have a delta close to -.50. It is important to be aware of the delta so you can gauge the value the option will increase or decrease with changes in the stock price.

This concept also applies to theta. Understanding how much value the option will lose as time passes is important when monitoring the position, but it is not the most essential criteria to screen when looking for potential trades. Once again, as you become a more active options investor you will develop your own ranges for delta and theta based on your experience from previous trades.

SCREENING CAPABILITY

Throughout this chapter we have said to "screen for a percent to break even of X" and "Aggressive investors might look for a minimum percent naked yield of Y." We have also mentioned searching for minimum or maximum values for various other criteria when searching for a conservative, moderate, or aggressive type of naked put trade.

In Chapter 3, we introduced the patented SmartSearchXL tool as an essential tool to find only those potential trades that match your personal risk-reward tolerance. The SmartSearchXL tool will allow you to enter your desired criteria for the underlying stock, the naked put return criteria, and the risk assessment parameters that you want to see. This is a very powerful tool that will save you a lot of time when you are researching and analyzing new trades.

The SmartSearchXL tool will allow you to screen for more than 20 different fundamental and technical stock criteria while at the same time filter the results using more than 20 different option risk and reward criteria as well.

You will not need to enter criteria ranges for every possible filter that is available, as this would make the search too restrictive. The SmartSearchXL tool is designed so almost every investor can input a criteria set and find only those trades that best suit a personal investment strategy. Once you have decided if you wish to be conservative, moderate, or aggressive with your trading style, you simply input the values for return and risk aversion that you desire. In less than a second, the SmartSearchXL tool will find only those trades that match your criteria.

Based on the values that were discussed previously in this chapter, here are some guidelines you might want to consider to help you get started:

Conservative Investment Criteria (Lower Return, Higher Protection)
Percent Naked Yield greater than 0.5%
Percent to Break Even greater than 10%
Percent OTM greater than 10%
Implied Volatility less than 0.60
Percent Probability Above greater than 80%
Current Option Volume greater than 10
Open Interest greater than 50
Sort the results by the percent to break even value from highest to lowest

Moderate Investment Criteria (Good Return, Decent Protection)
Percent Naked Yield greater than 2%
Percent to Break Even greater than 5%
Percent OTM greater than 5%
Implied Volatility less than 0.75
Percent Probability Above greater than 70%
Current Option Volume greater than 10
Open Interest greater than 50
Sort the results by the percent naked yield value from highest to lowest

Aggressive Investment Criteria (High Return, Little or No Protection)

Percent Naked Yield greater than 3.5%

Percent to Break Even greater than 3%

Percent OTM greater than 0%

Implied Volatility less than 1.00 (or do not use a filter for IV at all)

Percent Probability Above greater than 45%

Current Option Volume greater than 0 (zero)

Open Interest greater than 0 (zero)

Sort the results by percent naked yield from highest to lowest

These criteria are simply guidelines supported by the information listed in the chapter. Once you get started trading naked puts, you will develop your own personal criteria set that matches your personal risk-reward tolerance. Using the patented SmartSearchXL tool, you will be able to input many different combinations of the stock and option criteria and be able to analyze the results of those combinations quickly and effortlessly. In a short period of time, you will have developed your own personal screening parameters that match your investment goals.

Now that we have discussed the stock and option criteria you can use to find the best trades that suit your investment strategy, we want to move forward and discuss the specifics of entering a naked put trade and the follow up techniques to track and manage your position.

Chapter 5

PLACING THE TRADE

WE HAVE PRESENTED YOU THE THEORY behind the naked put strategy. You have been introduced to a conservative approach to find, compare, and analyze potential naked put trades, and you have been introduced to the premier, web-based tool to assist in your research.

Now you can apply what you have learned, find the trade that best suits your personal risk-reward tolerance, and place the trade. What would the process be to place the trade?

First, you have to be qualified to trade the naked put strategy. Different brokers will have their own requirements and restrictions on which strategies you will be allowed to trade. Some requirements may include:

- Available funds or capital in your account

- Personal net worth

- Trading experience (stocks or mutual funds)

- Options trading experience

Other trading restrictions are based on the type of account you have. For example, in a retirement account, you may be limited as to the number of strategies your broker will allow you to trade. Some brokerage houses will only allow you to trade covered calls, long options, and naked puts in an IRA account.

If you have a cash or margin account, you will be able to trade a wider range of strategies, but you will have to apply to receive the upper level qualifications. Although each broker will have different requirements, here is a general look at the different strategies available in some trading levels:

- Level I – Buy stocks, mutual funds, short stock, and trade covered calls.

- Level II – Buy calls, buy puts, trade covered puts, and naked puts.

- Level III – Debit spreads, calendar call or put spreads, and long straddles.

- Level IV – Credit spreads and naked calls.

- Other Levels – Some brokerage houses may have a higher level for selling naked calls, as they are a riskier strategy.

If you are not sure you are approved or able to trade naked puts, contact your broker and inquire about any requirements to trade this strategy. If you need to apply for a higher level to trade naked puts, contact your broker and ask where you can find the forms to apply for the necessary level of options trading. (We assume that since you have purchased this text, you are already qualified to trade the naked put strategy or you are in the process of getting approved to trade this strategy.)

When you apply for approval to trade options, you will receive a pamphlet from the OCC (Options Clearing Corporation) called "Characteristics and Risks of Standardized Options." It is important that you read the information in that pamphlet to become familiar with the different aspects of assignment and exercise as well as the industries policies regarding options investing. You can quickly access this information and the most recent supplements at *http:// www.optionsclearing.com/publications/risks/riskchap1.jsp*

Or at:

http://www.cboe.com/Resources/Intro.aspx

TRADING OPTIONS ONLINE

In the early days of options trading, investors could only trade options on a few selected securities. Since options were a new trading vehicle and were lightly traded, the only way an individual investor could place a trade was to call the broker, who would in turn contact a floor trader to place the trade. This did not give individual investors much say in the premiums they would receive, and the *fill times* were fairly slow.

Today there are more than 3,000 stocks and indexes that are optionable, with more than 275,000 plus options from which to choose. Rapid advancements in technology during the past 15 years has made this process much simpler, faster, and more efficient. Exchanges are now entirely electronic and many brokerage houses have implemented online tools to enable investors to trade options with a simple click of a mouse. There are also several online options brokerage houses that offer discounted options commissions and online tools designed specifically for the active options investor.

With the increase of simplicity there also comes the possibility of making a simple mistake when placing a trade. If you click the wrong button, you may accidentally turn a bullish trade into a bearish trade or turn a position with a $500 maximum risk into a position with a $5,000 maximum risk.

Cannot happen, right? Unfortunately it does happen. Just think how many times you entered the wrong user id or password when accessing your e-mail account or brokerage account. Mistakes can happen. We have heard dozens of stories about investors who accidentally selected *"Buy to Open"* when they meant to click *"Sell to Open."* Sometimes the erroneous trade would suffer only a minimal loss as the investor could recover the mistake quickly. Other times the stock went quickly in the direction the investor wanted it to, but since the investor had entered the wrong trade, a significant amount of capital was lost. It is possible that the stock could move in a favorable direction if the trade was entered incorrectly; but, if we follow the trend of Murphy's Law, when a mistake is made, it typically will affect us negatively.

We have also heard several stories in which investors intended to only sell 10 or 15 contracts, but accidentally entered the trade as 100 or 150 contracts! This mistake is usually quite visible and can be caught before the trade is placed. Also, if you did not have enough capital in your account to cover that large of a trade, you would be alerted on the entry page that you would be unable to place the trade without more funds becoming available in the account.

To avoid these mistakes, make sure you know the basics of entering the naked put trade and be thoroughly familiar with your broker's trade-entry page. If your broker allows you to paper-trade, it is always a good idea to practice. This will not only give you confidence in the use of the trade-entry interface, it can also help build confidence before you place your first few trades.

Though there are hundreds of different brokers, the trade-entry interfaces should be fairly similar. When you log on to your account, you will have various links to your portfolio overview, account balances, trade history, open trades that have yet to be filled, and links you can click to make a trade. You may have links that will allow you "Trade Stocks" or to "Trade Options." If you are trading with a discount online broker who specializes in options investments, you may be able to select a specific strategy such as "Sell Naked Options" or "Sell Options."

Once you select the correct field, there are typically only four or five fields you will need to fill out:

1. Action—Defines the type of trade you are placing.

2. Symbol—Defines the strike price and expiration month of the put.

3. Number of Contracts—Defines how many put contracts you wish to sell.

4. Order Type—Allows you to place a Market Order or set a price limit.

5. Place Trade/Preview—Allows you to view the trade before it is placed.

Action—Sell to Open

Once you select "Trade Options" from your broker's interface, you still may need to clarify if you want to sell or to buy the option.

When you trade stocks you typically will have two choices, "Buy to Open" or "Sell to Open," allowing you to purchase shares of stock or short the stock. Your broker may use a drop down menu that allows you to choose which action you are taking, or your broker may use a radio button interface to choose between the two actions.

Regardless of the format, you will have the same two choices when you select to trade an option through your broker. To place a naked put trade, you would select "Sell to Open." Remember, you are looking to sell the put option to collect a premium and take advantage of a neutral to bullish security. If you accidentally selected "Buy to Open," you would be purchasing the put option, turning your neutral to bullish position into a speculative bearish position.

Symbol

Earlier we discussed how options are tracked across the exchanges. Typically, an option symbol will have five letters: The first three letters signify the security that the option represents, the next letter represents the expiration month for the option, and the last letter represents the strike price of the option you are selling.

Although the specific symbol that represents the option you wish to sell will be universal across all exchanges, the format may be slightly different depending on your broker. For example, let's say you were going to sell a July 30 strike put on stock ABC that is trading at $34.00. The option symbol would most likely be **ABCSF.**

The first three are the root letters and represent the underlying security, ABC. The fourth symbol, S, represents the expiration month, July in our example. The expiration letter differs between puts and calls. Puts have an expiration letters M through X, whereas calls are represented with expiration letters A through L. The fifth symbol,

F marks the option as the 30 strike. Keep in mind, some underlying symbols might only have one or two root symbols instead of three, and some stocks may have different root symbols than their listed trading symbols. If the stock has recently split, was part of a merger, paid a large one-time dividend, or had a similar event, the fifth symbol may be slightly different if the option has special delivery requirements (meaning the option represents more than 100 shares per contract).

Your broker may simply require you to enter the symbol directly as ABCSF. Some brokers may use a different format requiring you to put a period before the option symbol. If this is the case, the symbol would be entered into the trade entry field as .ABCSF. Other brokers may require a dash or hyphen between the root symbol and the expiration month, which would have to be entered as ABC-SF.

There are other possible symbol formats that are used. The key is to make sure you are very familiar with the specific format your broker uses to denote a specific option. If you enter the wrong format you will most likely receive a message stating the trade cannot be placed as the symbol could not be identified. This is easy to correct. What is not easy to correct is if you place the trade with the wrong expiration month letter or the wrong strike price letter. You might have inadvertently placed an aggressive ITM put trade instead of a conservative OTM put trade, or sold a put five months out in time instead of selling the near month put. Always make sure that you have input the correct symbol before placing the naked put trade.

Number of Contracts

Most likely this is a simple entry box in which you can type the number of contracts you wish to sell: 2, 5, 10, 15, etc. Common mistakes can be made in this field, but they are easy to catch. One time, I was placing a trade for five contracts but managed to hit the five button askew. I did not notice that the number of contracts the computer registered was 56. Needless to say, this drastically altered my risk-reward tolerance. I did not notice the mistake when I clicked the "Preview and Place Trade" button, but, fortunately, I noticed the error on the Preview Page.

As this is written, every online broker interface will allow you to preview the trade before you place the trade, giving you one more chance to review your trade before it is put into their system. Always make sure you have the correct number of contracts entered before you place the trade. Simple things such as double taps or repeated numbers can occur. If you enter an erroneous number of contracts that has a larger requirement than the funds you have available, you will most likely see a message from your broker that you do not have enough funds to place the trade.

Order Type

Although you have selected the action requesting to "Sell to Open" the put option, you still want to select how you want the trade to be placed. Some choices might include "Market Order," "Limit Order," "Stop" or "Stop Limit," and "Trailing Stop Loss" or "Trailing Stop Limits." These choices allow you to control the price that you receive for selling the naked put.

Market Order: This selection will tell your broker that you simply wish to receive the bid price that is currently listed on the exchanges. This type of order will get filled quickly, but there is no guarantee that the price you saw when you placed the trade is the price that you will receive. For example, you saw that ABCSF was trading at $0.85

when you started placing the trade. You enter the trade as a Market Order, but by the time you place the trade the option has fallen to $0.75 due to a change in the stock price. Your broker would sell the contract for you at the Market Price of $0.75, which would alter your potential reward and percent yield for the trade.

Limit Order: This is the recommended selection for trading options. The "Limit Order" allows you to choose the premium you wish to receive. You saw ABCSF trading at $0.85 when you began to place the trade. You know the percent yield this would potentially give you, which is one of the reasons you selected the trade. If you receive less than that amount, you are not really making the trade you wanted.

Also, we mentioned in Chapter 4 how some options may have a wide bid-ask spread. If you saw that ABCSF had a bid price of $0.85 and an ask price of $1.00, you may be able to squeeze out another nickel or two by putting in a limit order higher than the current market price. You could place a limit order to sell to open the put at $0.90 or $0.95. There is no guarantee that you would get filled at that price, but it is a possibility that you could get the higher fill price.

For example, a few days ago we sold a naked put against a higher-priced oil stock. The bid price for the OTM put was $11.50 and the ask price was $12.10. Ernie placed a limit order at $11.80, splitting the difference between the bid-ask spread. The order was immediately filled at the $11.80 limit order increasing the percent naked yield for the trade.

Stop and Stop Limits: These are more preventive steps that allow you to select a price at which you would want to close out the position. When entering a naked put trade, you would really only focus on "Market Order" or "Limit Order."

Trailing Stop Loss/Trailing Stop Limit: These are advanced methods that allow you place or close the trade based on the percentage or monetary movement on the stock. As you can usually satisfy your personal return and premium requirement using a "Limit Order," these methods should simply be used for protection and management techniques.

Market Open/Market Close: These types of selections are more for stocks than for options. Selecting this order type will tell your broker that you wish to sell or buy the stock or the option at the "Market Open Value" or at the "Market Close Value." Just like the "Market Order," this removes some of the control you have over the premium you receive for selling the option.

Duration: Whether you select a "Market Order" or a "Limit Order," you can choose the duration of the requested trade. The most common choices for the duration are "Day Order" and "Good 'till Canceled." The "Day Order" simply means that if your order is not filled during the current trading day, it will automatically cancel. The "Good 'till Canceled" will keep the trade request open until you decide to cancel the order. Some other choices are "Fill or Kill," which means you want to kill or cancel the trade if it is not filled to your requirements, and "Immediate or Cancel," meaning you want the trade to be canceled if it is not immediately filled.

Another selection you can make is "All or None." This simply means that if you cannot get filled at your selected premium for all contracts, then you do not want to be filled on any part of the trade.

Let's say you put in a "Limit Order" to sell 10 contracts of ABCSF at $0.90. Your broker may be able to fill half of that request at $0.90, but can only get $0.85 for the remaining five contracts. If you had

"All or None" selected, your broker would not sell the first five contracts even though you would receive the requested premium. If you did not select "All or None," your broker may have filled the first five contracts at $0.90, and you would still have an open order for the five remaining contracts. If they could get the $0.90 later, the order would be completely filled. If not, the order would stay open for the duration period you selected. Generally, commissions are based on the total order that you placed if executed in the same day even if there were two separate transactions needed to fill the entire order.

For example, let's say your commission cost is $12.95 per contract up to 10 contracts. You place a limit order to sell 10 contracts of ABCSF at $0.90 at 10:00 a.m. You immediately notice that five contracts were filled at $0.90, but you still have an open order for the five remaining contracts. At 3:00 p.m. that same day, the remaining five contracts are filled at the limit order of $0.90. Even though two separate transactions were needed to complete the trade, your broker would only charge you one commission of $12.95, not $25.90 for two transactions.

Once you have entered in your personal requirements, previewed the trade, and checked for errors, you can click the "Place Order" or "Trade" button to send the request to your broker. Once the trade is placed, you will be able to put in place certain management measures to protect yourself on the position. These management techniques will be discussed thoroughly in Chapter 6.

EFFECTIVELY USING TECHNOLOGY

You might be thinking this is a lot to take in and double check before you place a naked put trade. We just want to make sure you are aware of the possible errors that can occur so you can be better trained to avoid potential problems. In reality, your broker should have limited option tools that will allow you to place a naked put trade.

Most likely, your broker has a limited option chain that shows the various options available on a given security. They might show the symbol, strike price, current bid and ask price, current volume and, if you are lucky, the open interest and implied volatility for the option. This really does not tell you enough to make a fair analysis or comparison when making a naked put trade, but your broker will most likely have a direct link to an order page. If you click the correct link from your broker's chain to place a naked put trade, the symbol will be recorded into the entry field in the correct format, alleviating the possibility of typing in the wrong symbol or entering the correct symbol in the wrong format. You would still have to enter the correct action, the number of contracts you wish to trade, if you wish to place the trade as a market or limit order, and the price you would want to receive.

At PowerOptions, we have also simplified this process for you. We have shown you how you can effectively use the patented PowerOptions tools to find the best trades using numerous filters and data columns not available from a standard broker. Now we are going to show you how you can place a trade directly from the patented SmartSearchXL tool to minimize potential errors that might occur when you are entering a naked put trade.

First, pull up your saved search for the naked put strategy on PowerOptions or create a new search based on your current market sentiment. Then go through your analysis as outlined in Chapter 4. When you have found the trade or trades you wish to place, click the "More Information" button (little blue button) next to the listed trade. As shown in Figure 5.1, from the "More Information" menu, select "Broker Link," then select "Sell the Put."

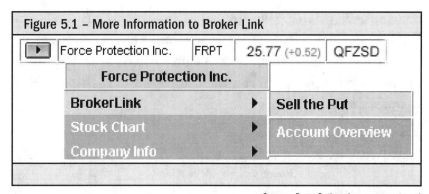

Figure 5.1 – More Information to Broker Link

Source: PowerOptions (www.poweropt.com)

This will link you to a secure login page for your personal trading account. In order to activate the Broker Link to quickly link your selected trades to your brokerage account, you must first request that your broker allow data from PowerOptions to link into your trading account. A complete step-by-step procedure for making this request is available in your PowerOptions - My Account menu under "Broker Link Settings." From the Learning Center tools, click "Broker Link Instructions" to view the procedure for establishing the Broker Link with available brokers partnered with PowerOptions (Figure 5.2).

Once you have the Broker Link set up, you will be able to link the data from the trade you found on PowerOptions into your trading

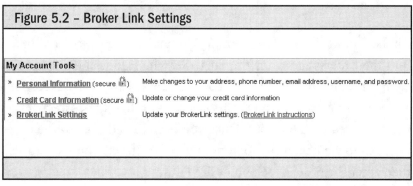

Figure 5.2 – Broker Link Settings

Source: PowerOptions (www.poweropt.com)

account. Select "Sell the Put" from the "Broker Link" menu, and you will be prompted to log on to your account. After you have entered in your log in information, click "Login" to access the order page. From this order page, you can enter in the specifics that you wish to trade.

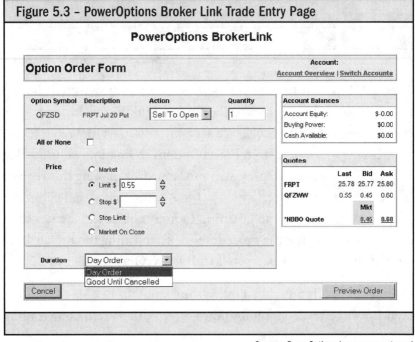

Figure 5.3 – PowerOptions Broker Link Trade Entry Page

Source: PowerOptions (www.poweropt.com)

As shown in Figure 5.3, the option symbol has been correctly linked into the order page from the SmartSearchXL tool and the correct action has already been selected. You ran a search for naked puts, and we have programmed the Broker Link so that the correct action is transferred over for you. Once you have linked over to the order form, simply enter in the total number of contracts you wish to sell, then enter the order type and desired duration.

Now that your information has been entered, click the "Preview and Place Order" button at the bottom of the order page. This will link you to the preview page (Figure 5.4) where you can check for any errors.

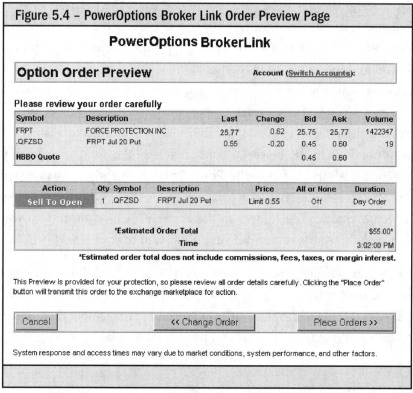

Figure 5.4 - PowerOptions Broker Link Order Preview Page

If you need to make an adjustment, simply click "Change Order" and you will be transferred back to the previous order page. Once you are confident that everything is correct for your desired trade, click the "Place Order" button at the bottom of the preview page. Your trade will now be transferred electronically to your broker. You can check back at any time to see if the order is still open or if it has been filled.

You can also link trades to your broker from the PowerOptions option chain, the "One Strike" (Search by Symbol) tool, and the "Strategy Search Summary" tool.

Once the order has been placed, you can track the position in your brokerage account, but we recommend also using the PowerOptions Portfolio tools to track and manage your position. The PowerOptions Portfolio tools have been designed to show you the total profit and loss on your position with constant updates as the market changes. You can also track Upper and Lower Stop Losses in the PowerOptions Profit/Loss Portfolio, view the complete history of your portfolio in the PowerOptions Historical Portfolio, and quickly review all positions using the PowerOptions Snapshot Portfolio or the PowerOptions Portfolio Analysis tool. PowerOptions also has a Sector/Analysis breakdown in the Portfolio Allocation tool so you can quickly see the sector/industry allocation of your total portfolio.

In the next chapter, we will show you how beneficial these tools can be and how you can use them to effectively track and manage your naked put trade while also outlining several management techniques to help you maximize profits and protect your naked put trade.

Chapter 6

MONITORING AND MANAGING YOUR NAKED PUT TRADE

NOW THAT YOU HAVE PLACED YOUR TRADE, do you look away and assume everything will work out as you had planned during the expiration period? Absolutely not. You will need to monitor the transaction to make sure the position does not go against you. Most brokerage firms, especially online discount brokerage firms that specialize in options investments, will allow you to place stop limits on the option just as you can with a stock. Placing a stop order on the position will give you some freedom, but you will still need to watch the underlying security so you can be ready to take action if you need to manage the naked put trade.

Does this mean that you have to sit in front of your computer screen every minute of the trading day and watch the price changes in the underlying security or the price of the put you sold? Of course not, but you do want to have the ability to quickly reference the price of your underlying stock, the put option, and the market in general.

TRACKING CURRENT POSITIONS

The best tool to use for this quick reference is a *watch list*. A watch list allows you to quickly view the current prices of the stocks that you have trades on, the put options you have sold, and the various indexes as well. Monitoring the larger indexes such as the NASDAQ or the S&P 500 will give you a quick overview of the market in general.

Figure 6.1 is the PowerOptions PowerWatch watch list tool. Once you have added the symbols you wish to track, you will get a quick view of the current price and the updated price change of the security or option. At the top of this example are the quotes for the NASDAQ ($NDX), the S&P 500 ($SPX), and the Volatility Index ($VIX) that measures the average volatility across the market.

Figure 6.1 - PowerWatch Tool

Info	Sym	Price	Chng
►	$NDX	$2,223.97	23.49
►	$SPX	$1,520.27	18.10
►	$VIX	$21.39	-2.92
►	AAPL	$191.79	5.61
►	DIA	$136.51	1.30
►	GOOG	$741.79	16.14
►	IBM	$113.17	-0.23
►	MSFT	$36.41	-0.32
►	QQQQ	$54.68	0.61

PowerWatch® List 3

Add   Delete

Source: PowerOptions (www.poweropt.com)

Next to each symbol is a "More Information" button that allows you to quickly link to the Company Information, Stock Chart, Option Chain, and Stock or Option Research tool, giving you an entire overview of all the fundamental and technical data that is available.

Watch list tools are very useful when an investor is looking for an immediate snapshot of the current market activity and the prices of underlying stocks or options. Most brokers will have a basic watch list capability.

Once you have placed a trade with your broker, you will be able to view the profit/loss on the position in your trading account. Traditional brokers only offer limited information on an options trade, though many brokers have updated their software to meet the demand of the growing number of options investors. Discount online brokers that focus specifically on options investing will have a wider range of tools to help you monitor your option investments.

The PowerOptions Portfolio tools were designed by options investors and enhanced by subscriber input during the last 10 years. These tools will greatly help you track, paper trade, adjust, and manage your naked put positions.

Once you have found a naked put that you are interested in trading or paper trading, you can manually enter the trade into the PowerOptions Profit/Loss Position Portfolio or link the trade information into the Portfolio tool from the various search tools using the "More Information" button.

Once you have entered the trade into the Portfolio tool, the values of the option and the underlying stock will update continuously so that you can view the most current value of the position. Figure 6.2 is a view of the Profit/Loss Position Portfolio.

Figure 6.2 – Profit/Loss Position Portfolio

Portfolio Settings	Portfolio Details
Select Portfolio: Put Positions	
Enter new position: Select Strategy	☐ Email portfolio daily
View Month: All Months	☐ View position analysis

	Basis Date:	4/13/2007
	Starting Basis:	$100,000.00
	Cash On Hand:	$101,085.00
	Return:	1.1%

Edit More Info	Notes Stop Limits	Issue Symbol	Description	Qty	Trans Date	Age	Net Cost	Issue Price/ Total Change		Curr. Price/ Change Today		Gain/Loss	Market Value
4 Short Puts													
▶	🔲	ASU	JUL 37.5 PUT [A @ $39.94 +0.32]	-5	6/17/07	(2)	-230.00	0.46	-0.42	0.04	-0.02	210.00	91.3%	$-20.00
▶	🔲	APASP	JUL 80.0 PUT [APA@88.78 +1.16]	-5	6/17/07	(2)	-225.00	0.45	0.00	0.05	-0.40	200.00	88.9%	$-25.00
▶	🔲	QFZSD	JUL 20.0 PUT [FRPT@20.43 +0.0]	-1	6/17/07	(2)	-50.00	0.50	-0.10	0.25	-0.25	25.00	50.0%	$-25.00
▶	🔲	IBMST	JUL 100.0 PUT[IBM@115.87+1.05]	-5	7/1/07	(2)	-125.00	0.25	-0.20	0.05	0.00	100.00	80.0%	$-25.00

Market Prices	Index	Price	Change	Net Cost:	$-630.00	Market Value:		$-95.00
1/100 DJ INDUSTRIALS	$DJX	$131.29	↓-1.37	Total Income:	$ 630.00	Cash on Hand:		$ 101,180.00
NASDAQ 100 INDEX	$NDX	$2,063.91	↓-42.25			Total Value:		$ 101,085.00
S&P 500 INDEX	$SPX	$1,461.34	↓-13.43			Portfolio Return:		1.1%
						Potential Cash Secured Put Obligation:		$ 110,750.00

Source: PowerOptions (www.poweropt.com)

Figure 6.2 displays the detailed trade information for your position. Starting with the third column from the left, the Profit/Loss Portfolio shows:

- *Issue Symbol:* The option symbol of your short put.

- *Description:* The short put expiration month and strike price, stock symbol, and current stock price and change today.

- *Qty (quantity):* The total number of contracts that you sold. (Note that the values are negative because we have shorted [sold] the put contract).

- *Trans. Date:* The date the trade was recorded into the Portfolio tool.

- *Age:* For options, this column shows the days remaining to expiration. For stocks it shows the number of days from the purchase date.

- *Net Cost:* The monetary value that was collected for selling the put.

- *Pos. Price:* The initial premium per contract that was received.

- *Curr. Price:* The current trading price of the put contract.

- *Chng. Today:* The daily change in the price of the put contract.

- *Pos. Change:* The difference between the Position Price and the Current Price.

- *Gain/Loss $:* The current monetary gain or loss if the position was liquidated today.

- *Gain/Loss %:* The current percentage gain or loss if the position was liquidated today.

The lower section of the PowerOptions Profit/Loss Position Portfolio shows the total incomes, costs, and return values for your portfolio:

- *Basis Date:* The date the Portfolio was created.

- *Starting Basis:* The original monetary amount in the account.

- *Total Costs:* The monetary amount of the current open trades. Note the value in figure 6.2 shows a negative $630.00. This is the premium received from selling the put contracts. If the put options had been purchased, this would show a positive cost value.

- *Total Income:* The total premium received from all open transactions (since this sample portfolio is only tracking naked put trades, the total income is equal to the positive value for the Total Cost field).

- *Market Value Sum:* This is the current liquidation value of the open positions. Figure 6.2 shows a negative Market Value Sum. The investor would have to buy to close the contracts in order to cancel the put contract obligation.

- *Cash on Hand:* The total amount of cash in the account. This includes the original starting basis minus any transaction costs plus any income that was received from selling the naked put (or any other income-generating options strategy). This value also includes profit earned from previous transactions.

- *Total Value:* This is the total value of the entire portfolio including the total cash and the liquidation value of all open positions.

- *Return on Account:* The percentage gain or loss for the entire portfolio. It is the percentage difference from the total value of the portfolio compared to the original starting basis.

- *Potential Cash-Secured Put Obligation:* This is the cash-secured margin value for the naked put transactions in the portfolio.

The PowerOptions Profit/Loss Position Portfolio will update continuously throughout the trading day with current market values, allowing the investor to easily monitor trades, individual position return, and total portfolio return.

The first two columns in the Profit/Loss Position Portfolio tool, the Edit/More Info and the Notes/Stop Limits column allow investors to manage and edit the position, link to research tools, and record notes for any transaction with stop limits on the stock or on the option. A more detailed description of these useful features will be discussed later in the position management portion of this chapter.

TRACKING HISTORICAL POSITIONS

An investor will also want to have a full access view to the historical positions that have been closed, expired, or assigned. This allows the investor to view past profits or losses as well as the overall return on an entire portfolio over time. Your broker will have a record of your historical positions and the closing prices, but the PowerOptions Historical Portfolio displays the information more directed to the options investor. Figure 6.3 shows the PowerOptions Historical Portfolio.

Figure 6.3 – PowerOptions Historical Portfolio

Edit	Notes	Events	Description	Cost Basis	Opened	Sale Price	Closed	Days In	Gain/Loss $	Gain/Loss %
Edit		Events	5 JUL 100.00 IBM PUT (IBMST)		7/1/2007	$125.00		22	n/a	n/a
Edit		Events	5 JUL 80.00 APA PUT (APASP)		6/17/2007	$225.00		36	n/a	n/a
Edit		Events	5 JUL 37.50 A PUT (ASU)		6/17/2007	$230.00		36	n/a	n/a
Edit		Events	5 JUL 25.00 FRPT PUT (QFZSE)		6/14/2007	$1,175.00		39	n/a	n/a
Edit		Events	1 JUL 20.00 FRPT PUT (QFZSD)		6/14/2007	$50.00		39	n/a	n/a
Edit		Events	10 JUN 37.50 GES PUT (GESRU)	$0.00	5/24/2007	$550.00	6/23/07	30	$550.00	100.00%
						Total Gain/Loss			$550.00	100.00%

Source: PowerOptions (www.poweropt.com)

In the Historical Portfolio, you can select to view closed positions or all positions together. The Historical Portfolio will record the full trade description, the open and closing date of the position, the total number of trading days, and the gain or loss on the closed positions.

You can edit the positions and record trade notes, as well as enter past positions that have been traded, giving you an accurate monetary value in the Profit/Loss Position Portfolio. The Historical Portfolio is a very useful tool for organizing your yearly profits on an individual security when you are preparing for tax season. It allows you to view closed transactions by individual tax year and it is ordered by the transaction date. The Historical Portfolio tool was designed to have the same order and arrangement as a Schedule D form.

Referring back to Figure 6.2, the original starting basis was $100,000. The current income received from the open trades was $630.00. This would lead us to assume that the cash on hand for the portfolio would be $100,630. However, the cash on hand value was $101,180. The additional $550 in cash came from a previous expired position on GES, which is shown on the last line of Figure 6.2.

On May 24, 2006, 10 contracts of the GES June 37.5 strike put were sold for a total value of $550. The put expired worthless on June 23 and the $550 premium was kept. This past profit added to the current income received from the open positions accounts for the cash on hand value in the Profit/Loss Portfolio.

This closed position was recorded into the Historical Portfolio automatically. If you are using the PowerOptions Profit/Loss Position Portfolio to paper trade or track your positions, you can easily manage those positions using the "Edit/More Information" buttons shown in Figure 6.4. Simply click the "Edit/More Info" button next to the position and select "Position Options." You will have a wide range of choices to manage the trade:

- Edit Position—Edit the price or trade date.

- Close this Leg—Enter in your buy back cost. This will record the trade automatically in the Historical Portfolio.

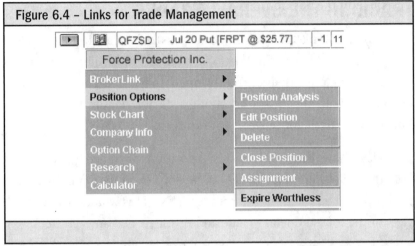

Figure 6.4 – Links for Trade Management

| | | QFZSD | Jul 20 Put [FRPT @ $25.77] | -1 | 11 |

Force Protection Inc.

BrokerLink ▶
Position Options ▶ → Position Analysis
Stock Chart ▶ Edit Position
Company Info ▶ Delete
Option Chain Close Position
Research ▶ Assignment
Calculator Expire Worthless

Source: PowerOptions (www.poweropt.com)

- Expire Worthless—Reflects the option expired and the entire premium was kept. This will also automatically record the position in the Historical Portfolio tool.

- Assignment—Would reflect that the put was assigned and the investor purchased shares of stock to fulfill the obligation. The shares would appear in the Profit/Loss Position Portfolio as "Long Stock."

- Delete—If you were paper trading a certain strategy or methodology and decided to start over, you could simply use the "Delete" function to remove the position from the record. All costs or premiums received would also be deleted from the cash on hand value and income values.

Using the "More Info" button to reflect the management techniques, expired or assigned options will greatly help you correctly track all the profits or losses on all of your paper trades or actual positions.

TRACKING THE OVERALL TRADES

There are other useful tools that can be used for tracking your naked put positions. First is the Portfolio Analysis tool. This tool breaks down all trades, either currently open in your account or previously closed, arranged by underlying security. Figure 6.5 shows the Portfolio Analysis for our current portfolio.

This view shows the open and closed positions arranged by stock symbol. If we had sold puts on GES for various expiration months, those trades would be listed in order under GES. This would give us a full view of the total monetary value and profit earned on each stock.

A second tool that can be very useful for viewing the allocation of your overall portfolio is the Sector/Industry Allocation Analysis tool. This allows you to view your asset allocation arranged by investment amount, position value, or total number of positions.

Figure 6.5 – Portfolio Analysis Tool

Description	Type	Cost Basis	Opened	Sale Price	Closed	Days	Gain/Loss $	%
A								
5 JUL 37.50 PUT (ASU)	O	$20.00		$ 230.00		31	$210.00	91.3%
				Total Gain/Loss for A			$210.00	1,050%
APA								
5 JUL 80 PUT (APASP)	O	$25.00	6/17/07	$ 225.00		35	$200.00	88.9%
				Total Gain/Loss for APA			$200.00	800.0%
FRPT								
1 JUL 20.00 FRPT PUT (QFZSD)	O	$25.00	6/17/07	$50.00		31	$25.00	50.0%
				Total Gain/Loss for FRPT			$25.00	100.0%
GES								
10 JUN 37.50 PUT (GESRU)	O	$0.00	6/17/07	$ 550.00	6/23/07	58	$550.00	100.0%
				Total Gain/Loss for GES			$550.00	100.0%
IBM								
5 JUL 100.00 IBM PUT (IBMST)	O	$25.00	7/1/07	$ 125.00		0	$100.00	80.0%
				Total Gain/Loss for IBM			$100.00	400.0%
				Total Gain/Loss			$1,085.00	1,142.1%

Source: PowerOptions (www.poweropt.com)

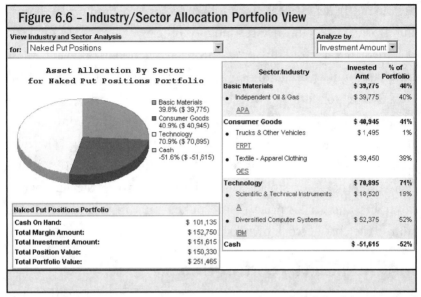

Figure 6.6 – Industry/Sector Allocation Portfolio View

Sector/Industry	Invested Amt	% of Portfolio
Basic Materials	**$ 39,775**	**40%**
• Independent Oil & Gas	$ 39,775	40%
APA		
Consumer Goods	**$ 40,945**	**41%**
• Trucks & Other Vehicles	$ 1,495	1%
FRPT		
• Textile - Apparel Clothing	$ 39,450	39%
GES		
Technology	**$ 70,895**	**71%**
• Scientific & Technical Instruments	$ 18,520	19%
A		
• Diversified Computer Systems	$ 52,375	52%
IBM		
Cash	**$ -51,615**	**-52%**

Asset Allocation By Sector for Naked Put Positions Portfolio

- Basic Materials 39.8% ($ 39,775)
- Consumer Goods 40.9% ($ 40,945)
- Technology 70.9% ($ 70,895)
- Cash -51.6% ($ -51,615)

Naked Put Positions Portfolio

Cash On Hand:	$ 101,135
Total Margin Amount:	$ 152,750
Total Investment Amount:	$ 151,615
Total Position Value:	$ 150,330
Total Portfolio Value:	$ 251,465

Source: PowerOptions (www.poweropt.com)

The allocation view is not only beneficial to view your overall sector and industry diversification, but it can also help with strategic management techniques.

The Cash on Hand, Margin Amount, Investment Amount, and Total Position Value have been transferred from the Profit/Loss position portfolio and are displayed in the lower left hand corner. On the right hand side, the current positions are arranged by Sector/Industry, showing the current Investment Amount for each position and the percentage that amount represents of the entire portfolio. To the left is a convenient pie chart reflecting that allocation information.

From Figure 6.6 we can extrapolate that our largest holdings are in the technology sector (71 percent of our total portfolio). If we were concerned about a broad market adjustment, we could use this information to protect the larger portion of our portfolio. Since we are currently heavy in the technology sector, we could research buying a protective put on a technology index or ETF. If the market declined in value due to some unforeseen geopolitical event, these purchased puts would counter some of the loss on the largest portion of our portfolio. (For more information on using index puts for portfolio management, go to http://blog.poweropt.com/ and go into the March 2006 archived blogs. Click on the blog "Portfolio Management: Stock Insurance." Although this article outlines protective methods for stock ownership, you can use the number of contracts and strike price of the naked puts in your portfolio to mimic the cost of stock ownership.)

MANAGEMENT TECHNIQUES

The most frequently asked question we have received over the years is probably, "Once I am in the position, what can I do if the stock goes against me?" Without proper management techniques or a structured exit strategy in place, an investor will experience a rapid decline in overall portfolio value.

There are two potential outcomes when an investor sells a naked put. First, the stock could rise and remain above the put strike price. In this scenario, the put option expires worthless and the investor keeps the premium. Second, the stock could fall below the put strike price and the investor will be forced to buy shares of stock. The question still remains, "How do we follow up a position if it expires worthless or if shares of stock are put to us?"

The answer to this question really depends on the individual investor's risk-reward tolerance and sentiment on the underlying security. The maximum risk on a naked put trade is if the stock falls drastically or the company declares bankruptcy, which is the same risk when owning shares of stock. The best way to outline the potential management techniques is to walk through the "What if?" scenarios on an example from our paper trading portfolio.

TRADE MANAGEMENT DECISIONS

Sell to Open 1 QFZSD July 20 Strike Put @ $0.50

Underlying Stock: FRPT @ $21.20

Trade Date: June 14 (expires in 35 days)

Our sentiment on the stock is bullish. We have sold the July 20 put as we feel the stock will remain trading above $20.00 in the next 35 days. We selected the 20 strike put after researching the chart and deciding that we would not mind owning shares of FRPT at $20.00, and the put also had a premium that matched our criteria.

Now, let's imagine that the date is July 15. We have been in the trade for 31 days and have four days remaining until July expiration.

Scenario 1: FRPT is trading at $20.43,
Put ask price is $0.25.

The stock has dropped slightly but still remains above the strike price. If you feel that the stock will remain above $20.00 in the next four days you can:

1. Leave the option open and hope it expires worthless.

2. Buy to close the option for $0.25. You would still retain $0.25 (50 percent) of the initial premium. Buying to close the put option would cancel your obligation.

If you close the position early or let it expire, you now want to reevaluate your sentiment on the stock. Based on your new evaluation of the stock, you may face three choices:

1. If you are still bullish on FRPT and feel that this was a minor correction, you could roll the position (called roll out) and sell to open the August 20 put for $1.85.

2. If your sentiment has changed slightly and you feel the stock may fall slightly below $20.00, you could roll the position (roll down) and sell the August 17.5 put for $0.80.

3. If you are no longer bullish on FRPT, simply take your profits on this initial position and search for a new stock that matches your criteria.

If you have decided to roll the position to a different strike price for the next month's expiration, you will need to recalculate the cost basis of your total position, the adjusted percent to break even, and the new potential percent naked yield. To simplify this process, PowerOptions has created a management tool that will help you with your roll out decisions.

Earlier in this chapter we mentioned the first two columns on the Profit/Loss Position Portfolio: The "Edit/More Info" button and the "Notes/Stop Limits" field. One of the most powerful features of using the PowerOptions Portfolio tools to track your positions is that you can link your recorded positions to the Position Analysis tool. The Position Analysis tool calculates your current position value, the potential expiration value (based on the current stock price), and calculates potential roll out opportunities for your position.

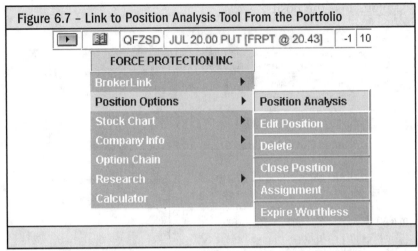

Figure 6.7 – Link to Position Analysis Tool From the Portfolio

QFZSD JUL 20.00 PUT [FRPT @ 20.43] -1 10

FORCE PROTECTION INC

BrokerLink ▶

Position Options ▶ | Position Analysis

Stock Chart ▶ | Edit Position

Company Info ▶ | Delete

Option Chain | Close Position

Research ▶ | Assignment

Calculator | Expire Worthless

Source: PowerOptions (www.poweropt.com)

To access this tool, an investor would click the "Edit/More Info" button next to the position in the Profit/Loss Position Portfolio. The investor would then select Position Options – Position Analysis (Figure 6.7).

This will link the position information, including symbols, premium, and commission costs, into the Position Analysis tool. Figure 6.8 displays the Position Analysis view for the naked put trade. The first section of the Position Analysis tool shows the trade information, break even value at expiration, current ask price for the sold put, delta, remaining time value, and the days remaining to expiration.

Below the initial trade information section, the position values are calculated with the most recent stock and option prices. This helps investors see the current value of their position, the current profit or loss on the position, and the percentage of the current profit or loss compared to the potential future expiration value. Figure 6.9 shows the position value fields.

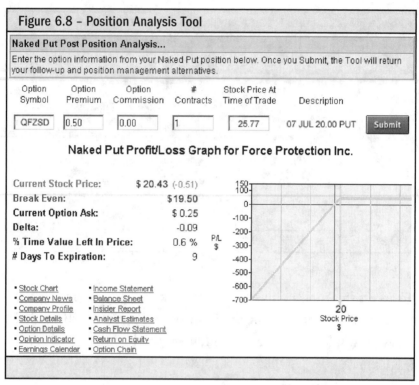

Figure 6.8 - Position Analysis Tool

Naked Put Post Position Analysis...

Enter the option information from your Naked Put position below. Once you Submit, the Tool will return your follow-up and position management alternatives.

Option Symbol	Option Premium	Option Commission	# Contracts	Stock Price At Time of Trade	Description	
QFZSD	0.50	0.00	1	25.77	07 JUL 20.00 PUT	Submit

Naked Put Profit/Loss Graph for Force Protection Inc.

Current Stock Price:	$ 20.43 (-0.51)
Break Even:	$19.50
Current Option Ask:	$ 0.25
Delta:	-0.09
% Time Value Left In Price:	0.6 %
# Days To Expiration:	9

- Stock Chart
- Company News
- Company Profile
- Stock Details
- Option Details
- Opinion Indicator
- Earnings Calendar
- Income Statement
- Balance Sheet
- Insider Report
- Analyst Estimates
- Cash Flow Statement
- Return on Equity
- Option Chain

Source: PowerOptions (www.poweropt.com)

Original Position Value: The original premium received from selling the put contract(s), the required cash-secured amount, and the expected percent naked yield. For the FRPT position, the original income was $50.00 ($0.50 * 1 contract * 100 shares per contract). The initial cash-secured requirement was $2,000 (strike price * 1 contract * 100 shares per contract). The expected return was 2.5 percent ($50.00 premium / $2,000 obligation).

Current Liquidation Value: The current buy back cost of the sold put contract(s), the profit or loss if the position was liquidated (Original Premium minus Buy Back Cost), the return on the position if the option was closed today, and the percentage of liquidation

Figure 6.9 – Position Value Fields

Original Position Value

This is the initial credit you will receive for selling the Put due to expire in 40 days.

Income = $ 50.00
Cash Secured = $ 2,000.00
Expected Return = 2.5%   Details

Current Liquidation Value

This is the expected value of this position if you bought to close this Naked Put at the present ask price of $ 0.25 per contract with 9 now remaining.

Current Liquidation Value = $ 25.00
Current Liquidation Profit/Loss = $ 25.00
Current Liquidation % Return = 1.3 % after 31 days
Liquidation Profit / Expiration Profit = 50.0%   Details

Future Expiration Value

This Put is out-of-the-money and should expire worthless. At expiration, the value of the position should be $ 0.00, and your profit is the original cost/original premium you collected minus the appropriate commissions.

Future Expiration Value = $0.00
Future Expiration Profit/Loss = $ 50.00   Details

Source: PowerOptions (www.poweropt.com)

profit compared to the expected profit. The current buy back cost is $0.25 * 1 contract * 100, or $25.00. The original premium received was $50.00, so the current liquidation profit is $25.00. The current return is 1.3 percent ($25.00 profit/$2,000), 50 percent of the initial expected profit.

Future Expiration Value: This shows the expected profit if the stock stays at the same price during the next four days (the days remaining to expiration). If FRPT remains at $20.43, the 20 strike put would expire worthless. The investor would keep the initial $50.00 premium received.

This second section gives you a complete view of your current profit or loss using updated market prices for the stock and for the option.

Following the management techniques outlined above, we still need to outline the potential roll out opportunities for the position.

Figure 6.10 - Roll Out Opportunity Field

Roll Out Opportunities...

Details

Here are some potential Roll Out opportunities for your OTM (Out-of-the-Money) Naked Put trade.

If you feel the stock is going to stay above the Put strike price over the next 9 days, you could simply let the Put expire worthless. If you feel the stock is going to continue up in price, you could Buy to Close QFZSD for $0.25 and Sell to Open one of the following Puts...

More Info	Put Symbol	Expire/Strike & Days To Exp.	Put Bid	Adj. Net Credit	Adj. % Naked Yield	Adj. % Naked Yield Annual	Adj. % Break Even	Prob. Above
▶	QFZTD	07 AUG 20.00 (30)	$1.85	$2.10	10.5%	127.8%	12.4%	53.1%
▶	QFZTW	07 AUG 17.50 (30)	$0.80	$1.05	6.0%	73.0%	19.5%	72.0%
▶	QFZUD	07 SEP 20.00 (65)	$2.60	$2.85	14.3%	80.0%	16.1%	52.1%

History...

Source: PowerOptions (www.poweropt.com)

The final section of the Position Analysis tool is shown in Figure 6.10. The potential option symbols are shown with a full description of the potential roll out opportunities. The current bid price for the new option is shown as well as the adjusted net credit, adjusted percent naked yield, and adjusted break even.

The first potential roll out opportunity is symbol QFZTD; the 2007 August 20 strike put that has 30 days remaining to expiration. The current market price of this option is $1.85, but the adjusted net credit is $2.10. Remember, if we liquidated the initial position, we would still keep $0.25 profit. That profit is added to the new option premium, giving an adjusted income of $2.10.

The adjusted percent naked yield is based on the new total premium of $2.10 compared to the cash-secured requirement of $2,000. The total requirement is the same since it is still the 20 strike put. The adjusted percent naked yield (annualized) is also shown. Remember, when comparing a possible trade in different expiration months, an investor will always want to look at the annualized return. The first line shows that selling the August 20 put would have a potential annualized percent naked yield of 127.8 percent, where the September 20 put (third roll out opportunity) would have a potential annualized return of 80.0 percent.

The adjusted percent to break even and the probability values are also shown to help the investor select the roll out opportunity that matches his or her risk-reward tolerance and new sentiment on the underlying security.

There is also a "History" section in the Position Analysis field. The "History" section would show any other trades that have previously been closed on FRPT. If we were able to continually roll this position month by month, our previous profits or losses would be reflected in the "History" field. Of course, you could only view that history if you had been using the PowerOptions Portfolio tools to paper trade or track your positions.

These analysis tools are designed specifically for the naked put investor and will greatly reduce an investor's research and analysis time, offering a distinct advantage in position management decisions.

But wait! There are other possible scenarios that need to be discussed.

Once again, let's imagine we entered the same example trade.

TRADE MANAGEMENT—TAKING PROFITS

Sell to Open 1 QFZSD July 20 Strike Put @ $0.50

Underlying Stock: FRPT @ $21.20

Trade Date: June 14 (expires in 35 days)

Today is July 15, four days from expiration. But let's imagine that FRPT is trading at $28.00 per share.

Scenario 2: FRPT is trading at $28.00, Put ask price is $0.05.

In this scenario, the stock has risen significantly. The sold put is essentially worthless now that it is so far OTM. The stock moved in our desired direction, which means we have the same two choices as we did with Scenario 1:

1. Leave the option open and let it expire worthless in four days (barring a sudden decline in FRPT).

2. Buy to close the option for $0.05. We would still retain $0.45 (90 percent) of the initial premium.

One management technique we suggest is if your option has declined 80 percent in price, whether due to time value decay or a significant change in the underlying security, it is never a bad idea to close the position early. This will allow you to lock in a large portion of your expected profits prior to the expiration date.

This brings us to another feature of the Profit/Loss Portfolio tool. The Portfolio tool will automatically alert you when any of your options have dropped 80 percent or more in value (Figure 6.11).

Figure 6.11 – Trade Alert Notification

Portfolio Alerts

Option Price Alerts - Possible actions to consider

* ASU (A JUL 37.5 PUT) has dropped 80% in price.

* APASP (APA JUL 80.0 PUT) has dropped 80% in price.

Source: PowerOptions (www.poweropt.com)

The prices we are using for this second scenario are fictitious. The FRPT 20 strike put does not appear in the Trade Alert section, as the actual price was $0.25, only a 50 percent decline in value.

Trading Tip: When trading income-generating strategies such as naked puts, covered calls, credit spreads, or calendar spreads, it is never a bad idea to close the position early if you have already made 80 percent of your expected profits. If we had sold a put for $1.00 and could buy to close the position for $0.15 prior to the expiration date, we would lock in 85 percent of our expected value. Another rule of thumb is to consider closing the position if there is less than 1 percent of time value remaining on the option.

In this second scenario, the stock has moved well above our obligation price. If we are still bullish on FRPT, we can use the Position Analysis tools just as we did in Scenario 1. Since the stock has risen, we may be able to roll our position to a much higher strike price, following the stock's upward trend. If FRPT was trading at $28.00, we may look to roll up and sell the August 27.5 strike or the August 25 strike put depending on our new sentiment of the stock. If $20.00 is still the target price for the stock, you could also roll out to the August 20 strike put. Remember, now that the stock has moved up, the August 20 strike put would have a much lower premium, as it is deeper OTM.

In this example, we were able to sell the July 20 strike put for $0.50 with 35 days left to expiration. FRPT was trading at $21.20 at the time of the trade, making the July 20 put only 5 percent OTM. Now that FRPT is trading at $28.00, the August 20 strike put is 28 percent OTM and would have a low probability of being assigned. This means the August 20 put would only have a $0.05 or $0.10 bid price. Depending on your commission costs, this might not be a profitable roll out scenario.

When the market rises significantly, you may want to roll your put options to the next higher strike price. As the stock price rises, your initial target price should adjust as well. You can still take advantage of the put premiums by rolling to the higher strikes, but you still only want to sell OTM puts. If the sudden rise in the stock price was due to an unexpected earnings surprise, a successful new product line or the expectation of further increase in the value of the stock, you may want to consider switching to a stronger bullish strategy such as long calls or buying the shares of stock outright.

We wish that all of your naked put trades followed the path of Scenario 1 or Scenario 2. However, the market is not always bullish and there will be occasions when the underlying security drops below the strike price of the naked put. This is when the management techniques are really important.

For the next scenario, let's imagine a completely different trade.

TRADE MANAGEMENT—MINIMIZING LOSSES

Sell to Open 1 QFZSE July 25 Strike Put @ $3.35.

Underlying Stock: FRPT @ $25.54.

Trade Date: June 14 (expires in 35 days).

In this example we are going to imagine that FRPT was trading at $25.54 on June 14. The target price on FRPT was $25.00 and the July 25 put was sold for $3.35. Once again, let's assume it is now July 15 and we have four days left to expiration.

Scenario 3: FRPT is trading at $20.43, Put ask price is $4.70.

Oops! It appears we did not correctly forecast this position and we are now facing a significant loss. As the position has gotten away from us, we again have two immediate choices.

1. Do nothing and let the put be assigned. We would be forced to buy 100 shares of FRPT at $25.00, our initial target price. FRPT is trading at $20.43 so we would have an unrealized loss of $4.57 ($20.43 current stock value minus $25.00 purchase price). Remember, we still keep the initial premium of $3.35, so the actual loss is only $1.22 ($3.35 initial premium received minus $4.57 unrealized loss).

2. Buy to close the put contract for the current ask price of $4.70. This would cancel our obligation to buy shares of stock, but we would realize a loss of $1.35 ($3.35 initial premium minus $4.70 buy back cost).

If you decide to buy to close the position and accept the realized loss, you are now faced with two repair choices:

1. Sell a lower strike put (roll down) against FRTP if you think the stock will recover.

2. Accept the loss on this stock and look for a new position that matches your criteria.

If the stock continues its current downtrend, then continuing to sell naked puts against the security may not be a profitable strategy. If you felt that FRTP was going to continue its decline, you could try to repair the loss by trading a bearish options strategy, such as buying long puts or selling a bear-call credit spread.

If your put option is ITM and you do nothing, you will be assigned and forced to buy shares of the underlying security. You will have to fulfill your obligation and purchase 100 shares of stock at $25.00 even though the shares are currently trading at $20.43. Including the initial premium you received, the position would be entered at a loss of $1.22. Now that you own shares of FRPT, you have a few choices to manage the position:

1. Sell the stock at market price and realize the loss of $1.22.

2. Hold on to the stock if you thought this was a minor correction and the shares will recover. The cost basis in this example is $21.65 ($25 purchase price minus $3.35 premium received). You would only need the stock to move up $1.22 to break even.

3. Now that you own shares of stock, you could sell a call against the stock entering into a covered call position (the *parity* trade to the naked put strategy). This is the recommended management technique if you let the put be assigned and are forced to purchase shares of stock.

Selecting the proper call to sell against the assigned shares requires some mathematical calculations. When you trade a covered call position, you are agreeing to deliver shares of stock at the sold call strike price if the stock is trading above that price at expiration. You will receive a premium for selling this call, but you need to make sure that the call premium you receive plus the strike price of the call is greater than your cost basis on the assigned shares.

TRADE MANAGEMENT—COVERED CALLS

Assigned 100 shares FRPT at $25.00.

Initial Premium Received (Naked Put) = $3.35.

Cost Basis = Stock Price – Premium = $21.65.

To turn the position into a covered call trade, you need to compare the premiums of the different calls that are available for the next expiration months. For FRPT, the August calls may be listed as follows:

Strike Price	Premium	CC Value	Profit compared to Cost Basis
17.5	$4.30	$21.80	$0.15 ($21.80 – $21.65)
20	$2.25	$22.25	$0.60 ($22.00 – $21.65)
22.5	$0.30	$22.80	$1.15 ($22.80 – $21.65)

The 22.5 strike call has the highest profit potential, but only if the shares are assigned at expiration. In order to be assigned, the stock would have to be trading above $22.50 at expiration. FRPT is currently at $20.43 and has dropped more than five points in the last 35 days. Even though the potential profit is higher, there would be a much lower probability of earning that return if the 22.5 call was sold against FRPT.

Selling the 20 strike call would potentially turn the $1.22 loss into a $0.60 gain. Since the August 20 call is ATM, there would be a 50-50 chance that the stock would stay above $20.00 and the call would be assigned.

The ITM 17.5 strike call only offers a $0.15 adjusted profit from the initial loss, but there is a higher probability that the shares would be assigned.

Turning your assigned shares into a covered call position can be a profitable repair strategy, but you might not be able to find profitable opportunities for every scenario. If the stock has dropped significantly, there might not be any call premiums available that will counter the loss taken on the initial naked put trade. You will want to evaluate which potential call matches your personal risk-reward tolerance by calculating the profits as shown above and analyzing the probability of achieving that repair return.

Our goal at PowerOptions is to simplify the option trading analysis and management techniques. The Position Analysis tool will calculate the potential covered call roll out opportunities for ITM naked puts as well. If you are using the PowerOptions Portfolio tool to track your positions, you can simply link to the Position Analysis tool to view

Figure 6.12 - Covered Call Repair Opportunities If Put Is Assigned

Details

Here are some potential Roll Out opportunities for your ITM (In-the-Money) Naked Put trade.

Since your Put is ITM you may be forced to buy shares of stock at $ 25.00 if you decide not to close the contract prior to the expiration date. Once you have purchased those shares you can now turn the position into a Covered Call trade to help recover any loss you may have taken on the initial put position.

You still keep the premium from your initial Naked Put write and you will also collect a second premium for selling the Covered Call. Your Cost Basis for the Roll Out opportunity is:

Assigned Put Strike Price - Initial Put Premium - New Premium from the Covered Call trade.

More Info	Call Symbol	Expire/Strike & Days To Exp.	Call Bid	Cost Basis	% Dnsd. Prot.	% Assnd	% Assnd Annual	Prob. Above
▶	QFZHD	07 AUG 20 (30)	$2.25	$19.40	5.0%	3.1%	37.6%	53.1%
▶	QFZIW	07 SEP 17.5 (65)	$4.30	$17.35	15.1%	0.9%	4.9%	65.4%
▶	QFZID	07 SEP 20.0 (65)	$3.10	$18.55	9.2%	7.8%	43.9%	52.1%
▶	QFZIE	07 SEP 25.0 (65)	$1.35	$20.30	0.6%	23.2%	130.0%	30.2%

Source: PowerOptions (www.poweropt.com)

these covered call repairs for naked puts that were assigned. For the FRPT scenario 3, the covered call repairs are shown in Figure 6.12.

The roll out opportunities for assigned naked puts shows the call symbol, expiration date, strike, and the days remaining to expiration. The current call bid is shown as well as the overall cost basis. The cost basis is calculated as:

Assigned Put Strike − Initial Put Premium − New Premium for selling the covered call.

The essential covered call risk and reward calculations are done for you based on the new cost basis:

• % Downside Protection—How far the stock can drop before you are losing money on the rolled position.

- % Return if Assigned—The return if the stock is trading above the strike price of the sold call and your shares are assigned.

- % Annualized Return—The annualized return if the rolled position is assigned.

- % Probability Above—The theoretical probability that the shares will be assigned at the rolled expiration date.

These parameters are the essential risk and reward values which will help you determine the best roll out opportunity that matches your investment goals and sentiment of the underlying security

The Position Analysis tool will look for profitable covered call opportunities up to three months out in time. The percent, if assigned, annualized value is shown to allow the investor to compare the returns over different expiration months. Typically, the far out expiration months will offer a lower annualized return compared to the near month expiration. However, from figure 6.10 we see that the August 20 call offers a 37.6 percent annualized return, where the September 20 call offers a higher annualized return of 43.9 percent. In this example, the September 20 call might be the better roll out opportunity. The September 17.5 strike has a high probability of being assigned but offers a relatively low return. However, it would still yield a profit repairing the initial naked put trade. The September 25 call offers the highest potential return but also has the lowest probability of earning that return.

Selecting which call to use to repair the ITM naked put trade comes down to the individual investor's risk-reward tolerance and reevaluation of the performance of the stock. The Position Analysis tool does not select which position is right for you; it merely does the math and displays the potentially profitable opportunities to save you time and help in your trade management decisions.

PREEMPTIVE MANAGEMENT

Although the PowerOptions tools showcased in this chapter can help you repair a naked put trade that has gone against you, most naked put investors will not enter into a trade without a specific exit strategy or management technique in place.

Even though you have done your research and have sold the put with the strike price that matches your target price, a sudden change in the performance of the stock (such as the example in Scenario 3) can have an effect on your initial sentiment. Here are some strategies you can place on your position to protect against large losses if the stock goes against you:

1. Set a stop on your position if the stock declines a significant amount. William O'Neill from IBD recommends closing a stock position if it drops 8 percent from the initial cost. You could use the same method, setting a stop to liquidate the naked put position if the stock declines 8 percent from its trading value when you sold the put.

   If you sold a put that was less than 8 percent OTM at the time of the trade, your put option would be slightly ITM if the stop was hit. This might still cause a loss, but it limits a further loss if the stock continues to decline.

2. Use the strike price of the put as your stop point. In Scenario 3, we would have closed the July 25 put once FRPT dropped to $25.00. The buy back cost might have been higher than the initial premium received but we would have limited the overall loss on the position. If your sentiment is still bullish, then let yourself be assigned and purchase the shares of stock at your target price.

3. A more protective method is to set a stop price slightly above the strike price of the put. This management technique might not have worked for Scenario 3, as the put was ATM at the time of the trade; however, it would have worked for the example trade in Scenario 1. In that example, the stock was trading at $21.20 and the July 20 put was sold. A stop could have been entered to liquidate the put if the stock dropped to $20.40 (a 3.7 percent decline in the stock price). Again, if there is a sudden correction, you might get stopped out early.

4. Throughout this text we have discussed the risk-reward tolerance of the position. If you do not want to risk more than three times the initial premium you received, then you can set a stop limit on the put premium as well. In the example trade from Scenario 1, the July 20 put was sold for $0.50. If we did not want to risk more than three times the initial premium, we could put in an order to close the option if the premium increased to $1.50. The only way that the put premium would increase is if the stock price fell or if there was a sudden shift in volatility.

Most brokers will allow you to place these types of stop limits on your positions. You can also track your stop loss settings using the PowerOptions Portfolio tool. Earlier we mentioned the Notes/Stop Limits column in the Profit/Loss Position Portfolio tool, see Figure 6.13. This section will allow you to enter in investment notes on the positions and enter in lower and upper stop limits on the stock or on the option.

Once you have entered the upper or lower stop limits the new columns will appear in the Profit/Loss Position Portfolio. If the upper or lower limit has been hit, the column will be highlighted, see Figure 6.14.

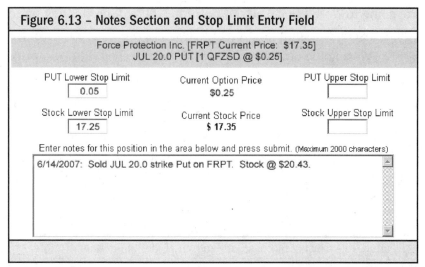

Figure 6.13 – Notes Section and Stop Limit Entry Field

Force Protection Inc. [FRPT Current Price: $17.35]
JUL 20.0 PUT [1 QFZSD @ $0.25]

PUT Lower Stop Limit   Current Option Price   PUT Upper Stop Limit
0.05 $0.25

Stock Lower Stop Limit   Current Stock Price   Stock Upper Stop Limit
17.25 $ 17.35

Enter notes for this position in the area below and press submit. (Maximum 2000 characters)

6/14/2007: Sold JUL 20.0 strike Put on FRPT. Stock @ $20.43.

Source: PowerOptions (www.poweropt.com)

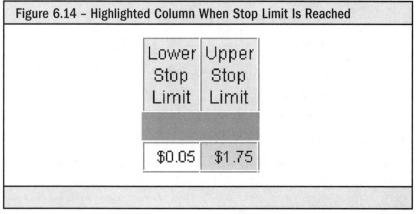

Figure 6.14 – Highlighted Column When Stop Limit Is Reached

Lower Stop Limit	Upper Stop Limit
$0.05	$1.75

Source: PowerOptions (www.poweropt.com)

In addition to the Upper Stop Limit column being highlighted, an alert will also appear in the Trade Alert section (refer to Figure 6.11).

These alerts will help you manage the position and alert you when an action might need to be taken based on your exit strategy. If you are going to close the naked put position, you will need to log on to your brokerage account and buy to close the open contract. When you are closing the put option, you will most likely pay the ask price of the put.

If you are using the PowerOptions Portfolio tools to track your position, you can use the Broker Link to close your position as well (Figure 6.15). Simply click the "More Information" button next to your position and select "Broker Link." You will then have a selection to "Close Position."

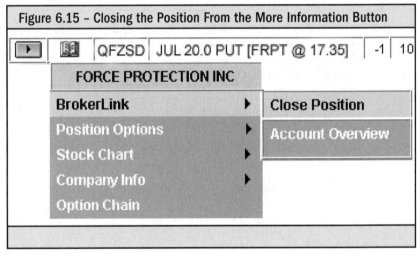

Figure 6.15 – Closing the Position From the More Information Button

Source: PowerOptions (www.poweropt.com)

Notice that the "More Information" button in the Portfolio tool also has links to the Stock Chart, Company Information, Option Chain and Research tools. These links will help you reevaluate your position if the stock has dropped significantly against you.

Once you have selected to close the position, you will be requested to enter your login information for your brokerage account. You will then be linked to your broker's entry page. This is the same page that was shown in Figure 5.3, only the default action would be "Buy to Close" since we are closing our open position.

As with the entry page from Chapter 5, if you notice a wide bid-ask spread when you are closing the position, you may try to enter a limit order to decrease your buy back cost. Be careful! If the stock is falling quickly, it is more important that you exit the position before it becomes too large of a loss, rather than trying to get a $0.05 or $0.10 cheaper buy back cost.

Once you have entered your order, you will be linked to the Order Preview that is identical to the page in which you were entering the trade (Figure 5.4). The only difference is the Action field. The initial trade was a sell to open action. The closing transaction is the opposite action: buy to close.

Once you have verified that the information in the entry form is correct, click the "Place Order" button. If you entered a limit order to close the option, you may need to check your account to verify the order was filled. If something has changed in the stock and you wish to get out of the position quickly to minimize losses, you may be better off simply entering a market order to ensure the position gets filled.

Stop for a moment and reflect. We have now completed the naked put journey from beginning to end. Let's take one more chapter to review the process briefly and showcase some real world examples of Group 1 and Group 2 naked put trades.

Chapter 7

REVIEW AND REAL WORLD EXAMPLES

THE PURPOSE OF THIS TEXT was to outline and define the ins and outs of the naked put strategy in a way to benefit the beginner, the intermediate, and the advanced options investor. The concepts discussed throughout this text detail specific aspects of the naked put investment strategy as interpreted by the authors, who combined have more than 30 years of options investing experience. This short chapter will review those aspects and reveal the real-world potentials of utilizing the naked put strategy to generate income in one's portfolio.

REVIEW FROM START TO FINISH

Chapter 1

In Chapter 1, you were introduced to options. Options are derivative investment vehicles investors can use to take advantage of movements in a stock without actually owning shares of the stock. Just like shares of stock, options can be bought or sold. An option contract typically represents 100 shares of the underlying stock. There are two types of options: calls and puts. Call options give the option buyer the right to buy shares of stock, where the call seller has the obligation to deliver shares of stock. Put options give the option buyer the right to sell shares of stock, where the put seller is obligated to buy shares of stock. There are various strike prices that an investor can choose to buy or sell. The strike price of the option represents the price the investor has agreed to purchase or sell shares of stock. Options expire on the third Friday of the designated month of the contract. On this expiration date, the contract will either be assigned, expire worthless, or the investor can close the obligation to avoid assignment or expiration. This text focused on selling put options as a way to buy shares of stock at a discount or to accrue income on a monthly basis.

Chapter 2

There are many types of investors who sell naked puts to generate income. When an investor sells (writes) a naked put, he or she collects a premium. The premium received is the maximum potential return on the investment and hedges the option seller against a decline in the underlying stock price. Selling naked puts allows investors to buy shares of stock at a discount or to profit on bullish to neutral stocks without owning any shares of that stock. Whether you are looking to buy shares of stock at a discount or earn profit from a bullish stock, you can still approach this strategy from a conservative, moderate, or aggressive standpoint. An investor needs to be knowledgeable of several factors before entering a naked put trade. These include: the individual's brokerage requirements for placing the trade; the obligations of the contract and the risks involved with the trade; the percent naked yield (the maximum return for the trade); the percent to break even (the protection for the trade); the theoretical probability of success on the trade; the pricing components that are included in the option premium; and, the volatility of the stock and how that affects the option premium and the risk of the potential trade.

Chapter 3

The naked put strategy is a neutral to bullish investment strategy; therefore, you want to find stocks that are neutral to bullish. You can use both fundamental and technical criteria to help find these types of stock. Look for stocks that have a rising chart pattern and good management as determined by evaluating the company's earnings, sales growth, new product lines, institutional holdings, and broker recommendations. Also look at the price of the stock compared to a short-term moving average. Even though you might have found stocks that matched your personal criteria, you will still need to research the stock to see if there is any news or upcoming events that might cause a shift in the underlying stock price.

Chapter 4

The purpose of this text is not to feed you the fish; the purpose of this text is to teach you how to fish. However, you cannot fish if you do not have the proper tools. The PowerOptions suite of tools has the equipment available to fish out those trades that best match your personal investment goals, whether they are conservative, moderate, or aggressive. When researching a naked put trade, you must first evaluate the risk-reward ratios for that trade. The reward values for a naked put trade are the premium received for selling the contract, the percent naked yield, time value, and percent time value. The risk assessment parameters are the percent to break even, the percent out-of-the-money (OTM), the percent probability above, and most of all the implied volatility of the option. A naked put investor has to be realistic about the expectations for the trade and should not expect to receive a very high return with a very high protection and a high probability of earning that return. The risk-reward criteria work in conjunction with one another and the more knowledge an investor has of these relationships, the more successful the investor will be in investing.

Chapter 5

Check with your broker to see what the broker requires for you to trade naked puts in your account. Once you are qualified and have found a position that matches your criteria, you can place the trade. Most brokerage firms will allow you to do this online. When you are trading a naked put, you are "Selling to Open" a put contract against the underlying stock. This obligates you to buy shares of stock at the selected strike price of the contract that is sold. When you are placing the trade, you need to make sure you are not selling more contracts than you can afford. If you can only afford to buy 1,000 shares of a given stock, then you can only afford to sell 10 contracts against that stock. When placing the order, avoid using a market order unless you are very comfortable with the underlying security. You might be able to squeeze out a better premium by entering a limit order when selling a naked put. Once you have placed the trade, you may need to set stop loss limits on the position and monitor the trade through your broker and through the patented tools on PowerOptions.

Chapter 6

Once you have entered the trade, you will need to track the position monitoring both the stock and the option. One quick way to monitor the stock price is to use a *watch list* tool. A better way to monitor your position is to track both the stock and the option together, which you can do with the PowerOptions Portfolio tool. Once you have entered the trade there are three possible outcomes: the stock stays above the put strike price and the option expires worthless; the stock drops below the put strike price and you are forced to buy shares of stock; or you buy to close the contract prior to expiration, thus canceling your obligation. When you enter into a naked put trade, you should have a specific exit strategy in place to minimize losses. There are management techniques you can employ if the stock drops, but it is always a good idea to have a strategy in place to preemptively manage the position and minimize your potential losses. Options strategies do involve risk, and may not be suitable for all investors.

REAL WORLD EXAMPLE 1 - BUYING FEDEX AT A DISCOUNT

In the spring of 2007, we received a call from one of our PowerOptions customers. He had been trading options for a year or so, mainly buying calls and puts to take advantage of movements in the underlying stock price. He was not entirely happy with the results and was interested in branching out and learning more about income-generating strategies, mainly covered calls and credit spreads. The customer realized that he could have a better success rate trading the income-generating strategies while generating 3 percent return or more each month.

During the discussion, the customer informed us that in April 2006 his advisor had recommended to buy FedEx (FDX) at a target price of $105.00. The customer placed an order to buy shares of FedEx with a $105.00 target price and left the required funds to purchase the stock on hold in his account. During the course of the year, from

April 2006 to April 2007, the stock did not drop below $105.00 while the order was in place (FedEx did drop below $105 in August, but the customer did not have the order entered as he was on vacation).

For one year, the customer held the funds in his account to buy the stock but never got filled. This is the perfect opportunity for a naked put strategy. Instead of placing a buy order with his broker and leaving the funds sitting in his account, the customer could have sold the 105 strike put month by month and generated income against the funds that were just sitting in his account. The customer was excited (and a little regretful) when we used the SmartHistoryXL back testing tool on PowerOptions to show him how much premium he could have earned from April 2006 to April 2007.

Trade Date	Sold Put	Stock Price	Premium	% Naked Yield
April 27, 2006	May 105	$115.20	$0.10	0.1%
May 22, 2006	June 105	$110.05	$1.25	1.2%
June 19, 2006	July 105	$109.72	$1.60	1.5%
Sep. 18, 2006	Oct. 105	$107.58	$2.85	2.7%
Oct. 23, 2006	Nov. 105	$114.65	$0.35	0.3%
Nov. 20, 2006	Dec. 105	$117.58	$0.10	0.1%
Dec. 18, 2006	Jan. 105	$115.06	$0.55	0.5%
Jan. 20, 2007	Feb. 105	$109.62	$0.70	0.7%
Feb. 20, 2007	March 105	$118.29	$0.05	0.05%
March 19, 2007	April 105	$112.48	$0.85	0.8%
April 23, 2007	May 105	$107.94	$1.00	1.0%
Total Trades: 11		Total Premium: $9.40 per contract.		

If the customer had used the naked put strategy, he would have earned an income of $9.40 per contract over the course of one year. The funds that were left on hold in his account to buy shares of FedEx would have covered the obligation of selling the put contract in each month. At the end of this year term, if the stock were put to him at the $105.00 price, his cost basis would only be $95.60. This would have allowed the customer to earn a monthly income and purchase shares of stock at a significant discount. This is the perfect example for the Group 1 naked put investor. If you are considering buying shares of stock at a set price, make your money work for you. Consider selling a naked put against that stock instead of simply placing a buy order with your broker. This will generate monthly income and allow you to buy shares of your stock at a discounted price.

REAL WORLD EXAMPLE 2 – BACK TESTING THE NAKED PUT CRITERIA

In Chapter 4, we outlined some specific criteria investors can use to help them identify conservative, moderate, and aggressive naked put trades. Using the SmartHistoryXL back testing tool, we can run these criteria and see the monthly return and total profit that could have been generated for each criteria set.

For these results, we searched for positions that matched the criteria on the Monday following the previous month's expiration. For example, we searched for positions on September 18, 2006, which was the Monday following September's expiration date. All three searches were looking for positions with less than 45 days until expiration. To be realistic, we only analyzed the top 20 trades that fit our search criteria. True, most investors would not make that many naked put trades in a given month, but for the months that had more than 30 or 40 results, we thought it best to just focus on the top 20. In all three searches there were several months that did not have 20 trades that matched the search parameters.

These results assume that no management techniques were applied to the positions and all naked put trades were held to expiration. For all three searches, we also looked only for stocks that had a minimum 5 percent earnings per share growth (EPSG), a broker recommendation of less than 3 (showing only those stocks that are a hold, buy, or strong buy recommendation), and we only looked for stocks that were currently trading above their 50-day moving average.

Conservative Criteria:

Percent Naked Yield greater than 0.5%
Percent to Break Even greater than 10%
Percent OTM greater than 10%
Implied Volatility less than 0.60
Percent Probability Above greater than 80%
Current Option Volume greater than 10
Open Interest greater than 50
Sort the results by the percent to break even value from highest to lowest.

Conservative Criteria Results:

Success Rate: 93%
Total Annual Return: 6.2%
Average Monthly Return: 0.52%

From April 2006 to expiration on April 2007, there were a total of 233 trades that matched the conservative parameters. Of those, 216 trades were successful, meaning the stock remained above the strike price and the put option expired worthless. This is a 93 percent success rate (216/233). The total return over the 12-month period was 6.2 percent, with an average monthly return of 0.52 percent. The highest monthly return was 1.3 percent (September to October positions) and the lowest monthly return was −0.3 percent (December 2006 to January 2007). The highest single position return was 2.1 percent in the September to October expiration period. The largest single position loss was −12.8% for NovaStar Financial during the December 2006 to January 2007 expiration period. The December 2006 to January 2007 expiration period was the only month that had a negative total return for the conservative criteria set.

Moderate Criteria:

Percent Naked Yield greater than 2%
Percent to Break Even greater than 5%
Percent OTM greater than 5%
Implied Volatility less than 0.75
Percent Probability Above greater than 70%
Current Option Volume greater than 10
Open Interest greater than 50
Sort the results by the percent naked yield value from highest to lowest.

Moderate Criteria Results:

Success Rate: 83%
Total Annual Return: 10.4%
Average Monthly Return: 0.87%

From April 2006 to expiration on April 2007, there were a total of 83 trades that matched the moderate parameters. Of those, 69 trades were successful, meaning the stock remained above the strike price and the put option expired worthless. This is an 83 percent success rate (69/83). The total return over the 12-month period was 10.4 percent, with an average monthly return of 0.87 percent. The highest monthly return was 2.8 percent (March 2007 to April 2007 positions) and the lowest monthly return was –3.5 percent (April 2006 to May 2006). The highest single position return was 3.2 percent in the March 2007 to April 2007 expiration period. The largest single position loss was –17.2 percent during the September 2006 to October 2006 expiration period. Four of the 12 expiration periods were losses ranging from –3.5 percent to –0.8 percent.

Aggressive Criteria:

Percent Naked Yield greater than 3.5%

Percent to Break Even greater than 3%

Percent OTM greater than 0%

Implied Volatility less than 1.00 (or do not use a filter for IV at all)

Percent Probability Above greater than 45%

Current Option Volume greater than 0

Open Interest greater than 0

Sort the results by percent naked yield from highest to lowest.

Aggressive Criteria Results:

Success Rate: 69%

Total Annual Return: –2.4%

Average Monthly Return: –0.2%

From April 2006 to expiration in April 2007, there were a total of 184 trades that matched the aggressive parameters. Of those, 127 trades were successful, meaning the stock remained above the strike price and the put option expired worthless. This is a 69 percent success rate (127/184). The total return over the 12-month period was –2.4 percent, with an average monthly return of –0.2 percent. The highest monthly return was 3.1 percent (March 2007 to April 2007 positions) and the lowest monthly return was –9.9 percent (February 2007 to

March 2007). The highest single position return was 8.0 percent during the July 2006 to August 2006 expiration period. The largest single position loss was –35.2 percent during the May 2006 to June 2006 expiration period. Five of the 12 expiration periods were losses ranging from –9.9 to –0.4.

Table 7.1 - Success Rate and Return Comparison

Investment Strategy	Trade Success Rate	Annual Return	Avg. Month Return
Conservative	93%	6.2%	0.52%
Moderate	83%	10.4%	0.87%
Aggressive	69%	–2.4%	–0.2%

CONCLUSIONS

These results match what we would expect to see. The conservative strategy had a high rate of success, as we were specifically looking for positions with a higher protection (percent to break even). Even though there was a high rate of success, the average monthly return and the annual return were fairly low. The moderate criteria set still had a success rate greater than 80 percent and the annualized return was pretty fair. Keep in mind, no management techniques were applied to these trades to minimize the loss as the stock moved against the position. We felt it best not to track these positions with management techniques involved, as investors use all different types of management techniques (as outlined in Chapter 6). If we did apply management techniques to the back tested positions, we would assume they would have the greatest effect on the aggressive criteria results. Several positions in the aggressive set had a potential percent naked yield higher than 5 percent. Without management techniques in place, many positions dropped to a –15 percent, –20 percent, or even –35 percent losses in the different expiration months. We cannot think of any investor who would let trades drop that far against him or her without taking some action to reduce the loss as the stock fell in price. However, that is the true definition of an aggressive trade: high potential return with a higher potential risk.

These results were included in this text to give the reader an idea of what to expect and how the market can work for you and against you. Past results should not be used as a measure of guaranteed future success. Options do involve risk and may not be suitable for every investor. These three criteria sets are also fairly rigid. An investor could easily mesh some of the criteria from the moderate set with the conservative set to possibly get better results. One could also average the ranges of the conservative set and the aggressive to set to form moderate parameters to find potential naked put trades. As you become more active and more experienced in naked put investing, you will create your own search parameters that match your personal goals.

We want to wish you the best of success on your investments, whatever stock, option, and mutual fund or bond strategy you might use. If you have any questions regarding any concepts or material in this text, simply direct your browser to www.poweropt.com and link to our contact details. You can email our support team at any time (support@poweropt.com) or call our toll free support number that is listed on the site.

GLOSSARY

Action – Defines the type of trade the investor is entering. The standard actions when entering a trade are Buy to Open or Sell to Open. When closing a position, the standard actions are Buy to Close or Sell to Close.

Aggressive Investor – An investor that looks to trade positions with a high potential return, little or no protection and a slim probability of earning the potential return.

All or None – A type of trade order that can be placed to assure the investor receives all shares or option contracts of a potential trade at a specific price set by the investor. If all shares or option contracts cannot be filled at the specific price, then no shares or option contracts will be traded.

American-Style Option – This kind of option contract may be exercised or assigned at any time between the date of purchase/ write and the expiration date. Most exchange-traded options are American-style.

Ask Price – The price that sellers are trying to get for an equity or option on the open market. The ask price will usually be higher than the last trade price, since most investors are trying to sell at the highest price the market will support. The ask price is the most likely price a buyer will pay for an equity or option when placing a market order.

Assignment – The action an option seller encounters when the option buyer exercises their rights and the option seller has to fulfill their obligations. For a short call, assignment occurs when the call seller has to deliver shares of stock; for a short put, assignment occurs when the put seller is forced to buy shares of stock at the strike price.

At-the-Money (ATM) – An option whose strike price is equal to the price of its underlying stock. When the stock price is very close to the strike price but not equal it is said to be near-the-money. Near-the-Money and At-the-Money options tend to have the most time premium.

Average Stock Volume – The daily volume of shares traded for any stock averaged over the last 90 days.

Average Broker Recommendation – Zacks fundamental research provides data on brokers that rate companies from 1 to 5. 1 is a strong buy, 2 is a buy, 3 is a hold, 4 is a sell and 5 is a strong sell recommendation. The average broker recommendation is the sum of all the recommendations divided by the number of brokers that have an opinion.

Back Testing – The practice of using historical data in order to analyze past performance of a particular trading methodology. The SmartHistoryXL tool mentioned in Chapter 3 is a useful tool for back testing options strategies.

Bearish Sentiment – The sentiment that a stock or the market in general will decline in price.

Beta – A measure of a security's price sensitivity to changes in the market. Any stock with a higher than market Beta is more volatile than the market, while any stock with a lower Beta can be expected to rise and fall more slowly than the market. The Beta of the S&P 500 is 1; a stock with a beta of 1 could be expected to move with the same volatility as the S&P 500 average.

Bid Price – The price that buyers are trying to get for an equity or option on the open market. This price will usually be lower than the last trade price since buyers would like to pay the lowest amount possible for an equity or option. The bid price is the most likely price a seller will collect for an equity or option when placing a market order.

Bid-Ask Spread – The price spread between the bid price (what a seller is most likely to receive) and the ask price (what a buyer is most likely to pay) for an equity or an option. Both sellers and buyers will try to maximize their trades by entering a limit order for a value that is between the bid-ask spread.

Black-Scholes Model – The Black-Scholes Model is a theoretical pricing model for options developed by Fischer Black and Myron Scholes. It is based on 5 factors: (1) the underlying stock price; (2) the strike price of the option; (3) days remaining to expiration; (4) current interest rates; and (5) the underlying stock volatility.

Black-Scholes Ratio – By comparing an option's Black-Scholes theoretical value to its current trading price, an investor can assess whether the option might be overvalued or undervalued. The B-S Ratio is calculated by taking the trading price of the option divided by the Black-Scholes theoretical worth for that option. Therefore, a B-S ratio of 1.2 tells us that the option is overvalued by 20 percent. A B-S Ratio of .8 tells us that the option is undervalued by 20 percent.

Break Even – The stock price at which any option strategy or combination stock and option strategy has a zero loss and a zero gain.

% to Break Even – The percentage a stock can change in value before the break even price is hit in any option strategy or combination stock and option strategy. For the naked put strategy, the percent to break even is calculated by subtracting the break-even price from the stock price and then dividing that value by the current stock price.

Bullish Sentiment – The sentiment that a stock or the market in general will rise in price.

Buy and Hold – An investment strategy in which an investor will purchase stock, mutual funds or ETFs and hope that the underlying security rises in value over time so the investor realizes a profit.

Buy to Close – A type of investment action where an investor will buy back any option contracts that have been sold in order to cancel the fulfillment requirements or obligations.

Buy to Open – A type of investment action where an investor will buy into a equity or option contract to speculate on the movement on the underlying security.

Buyer – A purchaser or speculator of an equity or option contract.

Call Option – A contract that offers the owner the right, but not the obligation to purchase stock at the strike price before the expiration date. One option contract gives the right to control 100 shares of the underlying stock, until expiration, unless the contract otherwise specifies.

Cash Secured – When an investor keeps the entire monetary amount to fulfill the obligation requirements of a naked put or naked call position.

Commissions – The price a broker will charge for a equity or option transaction.

Conservative Investor – An investor that looks to trade positions with a decent potential return, high protection and a high probability of earning the potential return.

Covered Call Strategy – A bullish investment strategy where a call option is sold against shares of stock that are owned to generate a cash income. For more information, refer to Covered Call Help section on the PowerOptions website (www.poweropt.com).

Covered Position – An investment strategy where short call contracts are linked to ownership of an equal number of shares of the underlying security (covered call) or an equal number of purchased call contracts at a different strike (credit or debit spread); or, where short put contracts are linked to an equal number of short stock (covered put) or an equal number of purchased put contracts (credit or debit spread).

Credit Spread – An option investment strategy where an investor receives a credit for selling call or put options while buying an equal or different amount of call or put options on the same underlying security. If an investor sells call options and buys an equal number of call options at a higher strike price and receives a credit, the position is a Bear Call Credit Spread. If an investor sells put options and buys an equal number of put options at a lower strike price, the position is a Bull Put Credit Spread.

Day Order – A duration order that can be placed with a broker such that the order will remain open until fulfillment or until the end of the trading day the order was placed.

Debit Spread – An option investment strategy where an investor pays a debit for selling call or put options while buying an equal or different amount of call or put options on the same underlying security. If an investor sells call options and buys an equal number of call options at a lower strike price and pays a debit, the position is a Bull Call Debit Spread. If an investor sells put options and buys an equal number of put options at a higher strike price, the position is a Bear Put Debit Spread.

Delta – Delta is a measure of the sensitivity the option value has to changes in the underlying equity price. For every dollar of movement in the stock price, the price of the option can be expected to move by delta points. Puts have a negative delta. If the delta is -.5 then a one point increase in the underlying equity price will cause the put to lose $0.50 in value. A put option that is deep out-of-the-money (OTM) will have a delta close to zero. A put option that is deep in-the-money (ITM) will have a delta close to -1.

Downside Protection – For a covered call strategy, downside protection is the percentage that the stock can drop before the investor is losing money on the transaction. For covered calls it is calculated by dividing the option premium received by the underlying stock price.

Earnings per Share Growth – Earnings per share growth is a company's change in earnings from last year to the estimate for the next year divided by the earnings from last year, expressed as a percent. It is the expected earnings growth from year to year.

European Style – This kind of option contract may be exercised only during a specified period of time just prior to its expiration date.

Exercise – The action an option buyer takes to force the option seller to fulfill their obligations. When a call owner exercises his or her contract, the call owner will purchase shares of stock from the call seller. When a put owner exercises his or her contract, the put seller is forced to buy shares of stock.

Expiration Date – The date on which an option and the right to exercise it or have it assigned, cease to exist. For most equity options the expiration date is the third Friday of the designated expiration month.

Expire (Worthless) – The action when an option is out-of-the-money (OTM) at expiration and ceases to exist without any intrinsic value.

Fundamental Criteria – The financial values of a stock that are used to determine the strength or weakness of the company. Some fundamental criteria include earnings, earnings growth, cash flow and sales.

Future Expiration Value – The expected value of the equity or combination equity and option transaction at the expiration date, assuming the equity remains at the current value through expiration. This value is shown on the PowerOptions Profit/Loss Portfolio and Position Analysis tool for management calculations.

Gamma – The rate at which an options delta changes as the price of the underlying changes. Gamma is usually expressed in deltas gained or lost per a one point change in the underlying equity. As an example, if gamma is .05 the options delta would change .05 if the underlying equity moved one point.

Good Till Canceled – A duration order that can be placed with a broker such that the order will remain open until fulfillment or until canceled by the investor.

Greeks – Options criteria that measure how the instrument will change in price due to changes in the underlying equity, volatility of the stock or interest rates in the market.

Group 1 Naked Put Investors – A group of investors that have researched the underlying security and have a neutral to bullish sentiment on the stock over an extended time period. These investors use naked puts to purchase shares of stock at a discount.

Group 2 Naked Put Investors – A group of investors that are more interested in the premium and % naked yield return on a stock that they are bullish on over a short period of time. Group 2 investors are typically not interested in purchasing shares of the underlying security.

Implied Volatility – The stock volatility that is implied by the actual trading price of the option. The Black-Scholes model is used to back calculate what volatility must be to create the present price of the option.

Implied Volatility Ratio – A comparison of the option's implied volatility to the underlying security's historical volatility. This ratio is calculated by dividing the implied volatility by the historical volatility. Implied volatility ratios greater than 1 are used to help determine overvalued options, where implied volatility ratios less than 1 point to undervalued options.

Income Generating Strategy – Stock option investment strategy where a premium or credit is received on a regular basis. These include the naked put strategy, covered calls, credit spreads and others.

Index Options – Option contracts that are available on an index such as the S&P 500 index, the Nasdaq 100 index or the Russell

2000. Indexes represent a collection of various stocks and typically have a lower historical volatility as they do not fluctuate in price as frequently as individual stocks.

Institutional Holdings – The number of shares owned by organizations that primarily invest their own assets or on behalf of others. Some examples of institutional investors are employee pension funds, insurance companies, banks and university endowments.

In-the-Money (ITM) – This phrase describes where the underlying stock price falls relative to the option strike price. For naked puts, it is when the price of the stock is lower that the strike price of the option. For call options, it is when the stock price is above the strike price of the option.

% In-the-Money – This is where the underlying stock price falls relative to the option strike price, expressed as a percentage. For naked puts, it is when the stock price is below the strike price of the option.

% In-the-Money = (Put Strike Price – Stock Price) / Stock Price

Intrinsic Value – Every option premium is comprised of some intrinsic value and some time value. The intrinsic value is based on how deep in the money the stock is priced. For a put it is how far below the strike price the stock price is located.

LEAPS – An acronym that stands for Long-term Equity Anticipation Securities. About 40% of the optionable stocks available, they are traded under different root symbols than the normal option series and only expire in January of the next two years. LEAPS is a registered trademark of the CBOE.

Limit Order – A type of order that is placed with the broker where the investor can set what price they would like to receive for selling or buying an equity or option. It is recommended to use a limit order when selling naked puts so the investor can hopefully receive a slightly higher premium than the offered bid price.

Liquidation Value – The value of a equity, option or combination equity and option strategy if the position were closed. This can be expressed as a monetary value or as a percentage.

Liquidity – A term used to describe how often a equity or option is traded. For options, liquidity can be measured using the volume of the option or the open interest.

Long Position – When an investor is a holder of an equity or option position over time when a change in the option or equity would be favorable. If an investor is long on a stock, they hope that the price goes up. If an investor is long a put contract, they hope that the stock declines in value.

Long Call – A bullish strategy where the investor purchases a call option speculating on a rise in price of the underlying security, thus increasing the value of the purchased call.

Long Put – A bearish strategy where the investor purchases a put option speculating on a decrease in price of the underlying security, thus increasing the value of the purchased put.

Management Techniques – Methods that are used to help maximize the potential return or minimize the potential loss on an equity, option or combination equity and option position.

Margin Requirement – The amount of money an uncovered (naked) option seller is required to deposit or have available in their account to maintain and cover an option position. Margin requirements are set by each brokerage house separately.

Market Capitalization – The stock price multiplied by the number of shares outstanding. A commonly used measure of the size of a company since larger companies tend to have higher stock prices and a resultant higher number of stock splits.

Market Maker – An individual who sets the bid and ask prices for an equity or an option.

Market Order – A type of transaction order where the investor agrees to receive or pay the listed market price for an equity or option.

Maximum Profit – The highest profit amount that can be made on the option position. For a naked put trade, the maximum profit is equal to the premium received when the put is sold.

Maximum Risk – The highest value that can be lost on the option position. For a naked put trade, the maximum risk is equal to the break-even price.

Moderate Investor – An investor that looks to trade positions where some protection is forfeited for a slightly higher return, with a 50-50 chance of earning the return.

Naked Call – A bearish strategy where the investor realizes a profit by making cash from selling (writing) a call without having the cash investment of owning the stock as in a covered call strategy. While the stock goes down, the investor keeps the premium on the sold call.

Naked Put – A bullish strategy where the investor realizes a profit by making cash from selling (writing) a put without having the cash investment of shorting the stock as in a covered put strategy. While the stock goes up, the investor keeps the premium on the sold put.

% Naked Yield – The percentage return if the option is sold and the stock is not owned or shorted. The percent naked yield is calculated by dividing the time value of the option by the strike price.

% Naked Yield (Annualized) – The naked yield return calculated on a yearly basis. The return is multiplied by 365 and then divided by the number of days remaining to expiration. This is an important value to use when comparing naked put trades that have different expiration months.

Neutral Sentiment – The sentiment that a stock or the market in general will remain in a sideways trading range over a period of time.

Open Interest – Open interest represents the number of open option contracts on the market over the life of the contract. The open interest is a measure of how liquid the options' contracts can be. When there is little or no open interest for an option, it can still be liquid because the Options Clearing Corporation (OCC) will make a market for it.

Option – An investment vehicle that is a contract to purchase or sell shares of the underlying stock. There are two types of options, calls and puts.

Option Chain – A tool that allows investors to view various data points for all call and put options that are available on an underlying equity.

Option Series – The available option expiration months that an investor can use to sell or buy options on a given equity. There are three option series: JAJO (January, April, July, October), MJSD (March, June, September, December), and FMAN (February, May, August, November). Every optionable stock will have the near and next month expiration available.

Option Symbol – An option symbol is comprised of three parts. The first one to three letters are the root symbol for the option. The second to last letter stands for the expiration month of the contract. The last letter in the symbol represents the strike price for the contract.

Option Volume – Option volume is the number of contracts traded on the current trading session or on the last trading day in the case of a holiday when the market is closed. Both buy orders and sell orders will cause this characteristic to increase.

Order Duration – A specification placed with your broker to cancel the trade or leave it open based on the time frame you selected. Some examples include day order, good 'till canceled and immediate or cancel.

Order Type – A specification placed with your broker allowing an investor to select how they want the position to be filled. Some examples include market order and limit order.

Out-of-the-Money (OTM) – This phrase describes where the underlying stock price falls relative to the option strike price. For naked puts, it is when the price of the stock is higher than the strike price of the option. For call options, it is when the stock price is below the strike price of the option.

% Out-of-the-Money – This is where the underlying stock price falls relative to the option strike price, expressed as a percentage. For naked puts, it is when the stock price is above the strike price of the option.

$$\% \text{ Out-of-the-Money} = (\text{Stock Price} - \text{Strike Price}) / \text{Stock Price}$$

Paper Trade – A useful educational method an investor can use before placing any actual trades. Paper trading with tools such as the PowerOptions Portfolio will help investors gain confidence and understanding of the market before placing real trades.

Premium – Another term for the price of the option.

Price-to-Earnings Ratio – The stock price divided by last years earnings. The higher the P/E value, the more you are paying for each dollar of earnings.

Probability Above/Below – This is the theoretical chance that an option has of being assigned. Specifically the chance that the stock price will be above/below the strike of the option. This is commonly expressed as a percentage.

Protective Put – A protective investment strategy where an investor will purchase put options to protect their shares of stock from large declines. The put acts as insurance for the underlying equity.

Put Option – A contract that gives the owner the right, but not the obligation, to sell a stock at the strike price before the expiration date. One option contract gives the right to control 100 shares of stock, until expiration, unless the contract otherwise specifies.

% Return if Assigned – The percentage return that is achieved in the covered call strategy when the stock is trading above the strike price of the sold call and the stock is assigned. This return takes into account the premium that is received and any profit /loss between the stock price and the sold call strike price.

% Return if Assigned (Annualized) – The % return if assigned value multiplied by 365 divided by the number of days remaining to the sold options expiration.

Rho – A measure of the sensitivity of an options price to a change in interest rates.

Risk-Reward Chart – A graphical interpretation of the maximum profit and potential losses for a given investment strategy.

Risk-Reward Ratio – A ratio of the various risk, risk-aversion and reward values for a given investment strategy.

Roll Down – The process of closing a current option position or letting it expire, then opening a new position at a lower strike price for the current expiration month or further out in time.

Roll Out – The process of closing a current option position or letting it expire, then opening a new position at the same strike, one expiration month or more out in time.

Roll Up – The process of closing a current option position or letting it expire, then opening a new position at a higher strike price for the current expiration month or further out in time.

Sell to Close – A type of investment action where an investor will sell any long option contracts in order to cancel the fulfillment requirements or obligations.

Sell to Open – A type of investment action where an investor will sell shares of an equity or option contracts in order to collect a premium and profit on the desired movement of the equity

Seller – A seller (writer) of an equity or option contract.

Short Position – When an investor is a seller of an equity or option position over a time when a change in price for the option or equity would be favorable. If an investor is short on a stock, they hope the price declines in value. If an investor has sold (short) a naked put, they hope the stock rises in value.

Simple Moving Average – Moving averages can be used to gauge the direction of price movement in any stock. They are typically measured in 20, 50, 100, 200 or 250 – day ranges. For naked puts, an investor might want to look for stocks that are trading above their 20-day or 50-day moving averages.

Stocks Implied Volatility Index (SIV) – The SIV is a way to measure the Volatility of the Stock based on the average OTM and ITM options implied volatilities for the underlying security. PowerOptions averages the implied volatilities of the two OTM and ITM calls and puts for the current month and the next target month to calculate the SIV value.

Stop Loss – A type of order that can be placed with a broker to help an investor manage their positions. A stop loss will trigger a closing action on the open position if a target price is encountered.

Strike Price – The price at which an option owner has the right, but not the obligation to deliver the underlying stock. For put sellers, this is the price at which the investor would have to purchase shares of stock of the option is assigned.

Technical Criteria – Stock analysis criteria that is based on the movements and trends of the stock and usually interpreted through charts.

Theoretical Value (Option) – The fair market value of an option determined using a theoretical calculation such as the Black-Scholes pricing model. By comparing the actual trading price of an option to its theoretical value, an investor can determine if the option is over-valued or undervalued.

Theta (Time Decay Factor) – The rate at which an option loses value as time passes. An option with a theta of $0.04 will lose $0.04 in value for each passing day. Therefore, if the option is worth $2.73 today, then tomorrow it will be worth $2.69 and the day after it will be worth $2.65.

Time Value or % Time Value – Every option premium is made up of some time value and some intrinsic value. From its creation date to its expiration date an options' time value decays away and any value left is intrinsic value which rises or falls with the price of the stock. The percent time value is the time value shown as a percent of the stock price.

Uncovered Position – An option position where stock has not been purchased or shorted to cover a sold call or a sold put. Uncovered positions are typically referred to as naked positions.

Underlying Security – The equity (either stock, index or ETF) whose shares are represented by the option contract that has been sold or purchased.

Vega (Kappa) – The sensitivity of an options theoretical value to a change in volatility. If an option has a Vega of $0.13, for each percentage point increase in volatility the option will gain $0.13 in value. As an example, if the value of the option is $3.50 at a volatility of 30%, then it will have a theoretical value of $3.63 at a volatility of 31% and a value of $3.37 at a volatility of 29%.

Volatility – A statistical measure of the annual fluctuation of the underlying stock. The volatility is used in option pricing models to determine the fair value of an option. Generally, the higher an equities' volatility, the more inflated the underlying option bid prices will be. Volatility is one of the factors considered in the Black-Scholes theoretical option pricing model. Several time periods can be used to create this measure. The standard volatility that is shown on PowerOptions is the 50-day volatility.

Volume – The total number of shares traded on a stock or the total number of contracts traded on an option for a given day.

Watch List – A tool that is used to track the changes in the stock price or the option price during a trading day.

Write – Another term that is used to describe when an option is sold. Option sellers are also referred to as 'option writers'.

Z-Score – A measure of likelihood for corporate bankruptcy developed by E.I. Altman. Studies have determined that the following values have significance:

Z < 1.81 the firm is likely to go bankrupt

Z between 1.81 and 2.67 is marginal

Z > 2.67 the firm is not likely to go bankrupt

ABOUT THE AUTHORS

ERNIE ZERENNER

During a 30-year career at Hewlett-Packard, Ernie Zerenner forged a trail of achievement. He developed four patents, delivered six well-received papers, received an international award for his invention of the Fused Silica Column, and had an impressive list of industry firsts, including the first microprocessor-driven instrument in the analytical industry.

During his tenure, Ernie continued his lifelong fascination with the stock market, building a successful portfolio. When retirement loomed, Ernie felt it was necessary to switch his investing philosophy from seeking capital gains to creating income from assets owned. So he turned to covered calls, an options trading strategy designed to generate consistent income.

Using a calculator and the financial pages, it took 8 to 10 hours to find good opportunities. In an attempt to cut that time frame, Ernie and a colleague designed a program to scan the entire market and find the best covered calls. The time required to do the job dropped from eight hours to eight minutes. It was breakthrough technology that earned a patent and was the basis for a web site called PowerOpt. com that not only supports Ernie's covered call investments, it supports thousands of subscriber/investors in, at last count, 57 countries all over the world.

PowerOpt.com is still the largest subscription program of Power Financial Group Inc., the trading company Ernie established in 1997. Today, he continues to innovate and seek ways to help investors grow through options trading.

MICHAEL CHUPKA

Michael Chupka grew up in northern Delaware, his father a Ph.D. in chemistry and his mother a registered nurse. In his high school years, Michael was deeply involved with various service organizations, mainly Key Club, giving much of his time freely to others. He also worked part time as a manager of a local store between his obligations as an officer of Key Club and captain of the cross country team.

Michael attended the University of Missouri-Rolla, majoring in geology, micropaleontology and English literature. He left University of Missouri-Rolla and returned to Delaware with a hope to further pursue his studies in the field of paleo-biology.

It was during this time that Power Financial Group, Inc., was in the midst of a major growth period and was looking to expand its support team. Greg Zerenner, Vice President of PowerOptions and now President of PowerOptionsApplied, approached Michael with an opportunity to join the PowerOptions staff. It was Mr. Zerenner's idea that Michael's strong dedication to service combined with a knowledge of scientific methods would make him a perfect fit to the PowerOptions support team.

Five years and tens of thousands of PowerOptions customers later, Mr. Chupka has established himself as head of the PowerOptions support team and a recognized options strategy educator in the industry. Michael has written dozens of educational articles for PowerOptions, but this is Michael's first book co-authored with Ernie Zerenner, President of Power Financial Group, Inc.

TRADING
RESOURCE
GUIDE

RECOMMENDED READING

THE FOUR BIGGEST MISTAKES IN OPTION TRADING, 2ND EDITION

by Jay Kaeppel

With over 50,000 copies in print for the first edition, Kaeppel's insight has undoubtedly made its mark in the options world. Now, he strikes again with an updated and more comprehensive look at those pesky mistakes that traders continue to make in trading options. In easy-to-understand terms, he systematically breaks down each problem and offers concrete and practical solutions to overcome it in the future.

Item #BCPOx4941403 • List Price: $19.95

OPTION VOLATILITY TRADING STRATEGIES

by Sheldon Natenberg

Unlike price and time, volatility is the one element of the market that is virtually invisible to a trader. Thus, having accurate methods to assess this elusive aspect is critical to successful options trading. With advances in technology, options have swelled in popularity and traders have risked their fortunes without an easy-to-understand explanation of the important factors in separating profit from loss.

Now, presented with clear and understandable insight are option-trading strategies, formulas, and definitions. You'll feel as if the master of trading, Sheldon Natenberg, is right next to you, guiding you through this potentially complex world of options.

Item #BCPOx5127729 • List Price: $39.95

OPTION SPREADS MADE EASY
COURSE BOOK WITH DVD

by George Fontanills

Fontanills shows you how you can use option spreads to expand your profit opportunities while managing your risk. With this ground-breaking DVD and book combination, you can pour over every word of Fontanills' presentation—learning each important point in a step-by-step, layer-by-layer process.

Item #BCPOx5446423 • List Price: $29.95

OPTION TRADING TACTICS
COURSE BOOK WITH DVD

by Oliver L. Velez

In this unique DVD/course book package, you'll learn Velez's secrets to enhancing your trading skills through options. It includes a full-length DVD of Velez's famed *Options Trading Seminar* and a corresponding course book to ensure you have all the tools necessary to make money with options.

Item #BCPOx5440077 • List Price: $39.95

To get the current lowest price on any item listed
Go to www.traderslibrary.com

THE LEAPS STRATEGIST: 108 PROVEN STRATEGIES FOR INCREASING INVESTMENT & TRADING PROFITS

by Michael C. Thomsett

Unleash the power of Long-Term Equity Anticipation Securities (LEAPS) for increasing gains, limiting losses, and protecting your trading and investing profits. The 108 powerful strategies lined out in this comprehensible guide by author Michael C. Thomsett help you both to advance your investing and trading techniques and to achieve your financial goals. Real-world examples and graphic illustrations point out the main keys of this book. Not only are LEAPS a low-risk alternative to buying stock, they are also a great way to maximize your capital.

Item #BCPOx2529875 • List Price: $34.95

AN INTRODUCTION TO OPTION TRADING SUCCESS - DVD

by James Bittman

Thinking of testing the waters in options, but haven't yet taken the plunge? Eliminate your fears and jump in with the CBOE's top options trainer, James Bittman, as he introduces first-timers and fledgling traders to the exciting options arena. Bittman explains in concise, step-by-step terms exactly how options work, providing clear explanations and examples of the most common - and valuable - option strategies.

Item #BCPOx3502409 • List Price: $99.00

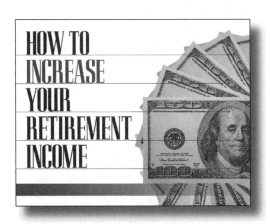

NOTES

NOTES

NOTES

NOTES

NOTES

NOTES

NOTES

NOTES